I0749804

TRUE STORIES
of Elmira, New York
Volume 5

By James Hare & Diane Janowski

This book is a selection of their freelance articles
in the Elmira *Star-Gazette*

True Stories of Elmira, New York, Volume 5

ISBN: 978-1-950822-09-6

Printed in the United States of America

First Edition

Cover image. Postcard view of Lake and East Water Streets. Publisher Rubin Bros,. Elmira, NY.

Dedicated to

Everyone affected by COVID-19

Be sure to look for our other books!

TRUE STORIES
of Elmira, New York

Volumes 1 , 2 , 3, and 4

By James Hare & Diane Janowski

Table of Contents

An illustration of Dan Noble, a 19th century English gentleman burglar, from "Recollections of a New York Chief of Police" (1887) by George W. Walling. Public domain.

A Person of Interest

by James Hare

He was described as an "athletic-built man, over six feet in height, had gray rolling eyes, and a light complexion. He was a jovial fellow and possessed a plentiful supply of ready cash, his entire energy being wasted in rollicking, carousing, and sporting, in which pursuit he knew not extremes." (*Star-Gazette*, June 19, 1928). Another account noted that he was a "pleasing fellow…in the prime of life, tall and straight, with sandy complexion and eyes which, though they had a slight defect, would look right through you, as one of his old-time friends put it." (*Telegram*, August 12, 1923)

He came to Elmira in February 1867, purchasing a home on the southwest corner of Grove and West Water Streets. His sporting activities brought him public notice. He gained a reputation as the "shrewdest faro bank player in the city" and a lover of fast horses. According to the Elmira *Advertiser*, March 20, 1895, "he had money to burn while the local sports could only light matches."

Dan Noble was a larger than life figure. The *Star-Gazette on* January 2, 1917, noted that "The Pinkertons and all other detectives who in the last 50 years have been guarding banks, always regarded Dan Noble as a man without equal. He never participated in small games."

Noble was born in England in 1834. His family moved to the United States when he was ten. Initially, a butcher boy, his shrewdness and skill led him to ownership of a "palatial saloon, billiard parlor and gambling rooms in New York City." (Elmira *Advertiser*, March 20, 1895)

The August 18, 1883, *Telegram* noted that "many stories have been told of how he fleeced the nabobs of the metropolis of large sums…

as a gambler he had few equals" and played "to obtain the wealth of the uninitiated, resulting successfully on almost every occasion."

Noble came to Elmira from New York City to escape the scrutiny he was under for "suspected" involvement in the Royal Insurance Company robbery on Wall Street, December 10, 1866.

Frank Knapp and Jimmie Griffin described the caper as "western hotelmen and sneak thieves" (*Star-Gazette* September 3, 1912) and Noble. Depending on which report one reads, the amount ranged from $275,000 to $1,700,000 in currency and bonds. Noble drove the get-away sleigh. Griffin and Knapp, posing as commercial travelers, entered the building, distracted the agent, and stole a tin box from an unlocked vault with the goods. The box was handed to Noble, who drove off to meet up later. BUT, according to the September 3, 1912, *Star-Gazette* "Griffin and Knapp went back to the house of Dan Noble, and there awaited his arrival; first easily, then anxiously, and finally furiously; but Dan did not turn up." By the time the company discovered and reported the robbery, Griffin, and Knapp knew they had been cheated, but could not say anything, so they fled to Montrèal. The police interviewed Noble many times, which caused him to relocate to Elmira to escape the heat. Noble's notoriety in Elmira caught Griffin's attention, who made several trips to this city to get his share. Not getting what he thought he should receive, he made a deal with the Insurance Company and swore an affidavit that implicated Noble in the robbery.

"He had money to burn while the local sports could only light matches."

On Sunday, August 17, 1867, Noble was arrested in Elmira and taken to New York City, where he was examined.

He returned to Elmira and was indicted.

The January 6, 1910, *Star-Gazette* describes the first of four trials in March 1869, "During his famous trial Dan Noble went on the stand in his own behalf, and during his examination made the following admissions as to his record, showing him to be quite a fellow: was indicted for stealing a watch and chain in 1860; indicted in 1859 in New York for stealing; declined to answer whether he was indicted at Troy for robbery...was arrested in Buffalo for picking pockets; was arrested in New York on election day for connection with a murder... and acknowledged an intimate acquaintance with many thieves and gamblers." He was acquitted on insufficient evidence. Ausburn Towner, working for the *Saturday Evening Review* of Elmira, wrote,

> *"Is it wonderful that a man who can reveal such a career should be popular in this city—some tell us the most popular man in this city!*
>
> *Is it surprising that the escape of such a man from the clutches of a heartless and mercenary prosecution should delight all good citizens and fill the minds of his jury with a pleasing sense of noble duty nobly done."*

Noble would be tried again in Elmira in June 1869, then a change of venue to Owego, New York with an October trial, both ended with hung juries. He was tried again in Owego in March 1871 and convicted and sentenced to Auburn prison for five years. However, the August 12, 1923, *Telegram* noted that "Noble still had friends in Elmira," and when he reached the prison, he got the best treatment possible with light duty in the hospital department. BUT, he did not like confinement, and on January 3, 1873, "with six others...he escaped.

A tunnel was excavated from the engine room under the wall and leading out to the river, and through this, they crawled, donned citizen clothes which had been provided by outside friends and departed."

Noble fled the country landing in Paris. While there, in 1874, he was connected with a diamond robbery. He was convicted, sentenced to five years but was able to escape after five months. He fled to Switzerland where in the middle of the night, he robbed a bank of $800,000. The August 12, 1923 *Telegram* wrote that he was caught, paid the bank half the money in return for a lighter sentence, and served four years. Upon completing his sentence, he went to London, where he purchased a hotel and gambling house outside the city. In 1881 he was arrested for forging $130,000 worth of bonds and sentenced to twenty years in prison.

In 1895, "he worked a pull through American friends who interceded and said he was dying in prison.

This brought his release...." (*Star-Gazette*, January 2, 1917). He returned to the United States. In 1897, after being arrested for passing a worthless check, he was identified as an escaped convict and returned to Auburn, where he served until 1899.

According to the January 2, 1917 *Star-Gazette*, "the last public record the police have of him was in 1907, when he was a complainant in the West Side Court, where he charged a woman with stealing his dog. He said he had merely allowed her to keep the dog for him, and she refused to give it up."

Dan Noble died at age 82 in 1916.

The old house on Maple Avenue circa 1900, photo courtesy of the author.

Sly and the Family Home

by Diane Janowski

The Sly family home at 300 Maple Avenue at the corner of Sly Street, was one of the first wooden structures in Elmira. Its demolition in 1961 marked the passing of a historic Greek-Revival home.

John Sly, and his wife, the former Polly Hammond, age 15, came to Newtown (now Elmira) on their honeymoon from Pennsylvania in 1788. They first built a log cabin in what is today's Brand Park. They dreamed of building a big house.

Across the street from their cabin, they did build their dream house in 1795. It was big, and that was a good thing as they eventually had thirteen children. John Sly owned more than 700 acres of the Southside. John was a farmer and grew tobacco. John and Polly were leading citizens in the old "South Port." The Sly family also ran the ferry boat across the Chemung River. Hence, the name "South Port." The Slys were members of the First Baptist Church in Southport. John was a founding member of the Chemung Canal Bank. Much of Southport was incorporated into the city of Elmira in 1864.

John died in 1856 and is buried in the family plot in Woodlawn Cemetery. The house stayed in the family. He left it to his daughter Catherine, as in Catherine Street.

With an extension of a right-wing and a new porch in the 1920s, the house had twenty rooms. Of course, the new extension contained an indoor swimming pool. Old furnishings in the Sly home included a beautiful old fireplace and brass fixtures.

In the early 1950s, the last owners, Frank and Pansy Ledford, of Big Flats, fell in love with the house and its giant elm in the front yard. They knew they had to buy the house. The Ledfords purchased it in 1953. By 1956 they were ready to sell. They soon found it was much too big for just two people. The taxes were excessive, and taking care of the house and grounds were too much to handle. They moved out and started thinking about selling the property around 1958. No one wanted the big house, and no one cared about historical value. To make matters worse, the beautiful elm succumbed to Dutch Elm disease and was cut down in 1960. Mrs. Ledford hoped to sell it to someone who would appreciate it. No one came, and the house was demolished in 1961.

The Ledfords went before the Elmira zoning commission for nearly ten years. The Mobil Oil Company was interested in the vacant lot. The zoning commissioners argued that there were already four gas stations in as many blocks. Finally, the zoning passed in late 1968, Mobil Oil quickly purchased the corner lot.

A gas station opened within the year. It was listed in the newspaper as a 24-hour service station/repair shop.

The newest version of the Express Mart (now called Speedway) opened slightly more south of its first location in 2003. Its construction took out three houses and a carriage house. Luckily, the carriage house was moved across Maple Avenue to the backyard of The Christmas House. It makes a beautiful addition to their backyard.

Sources:

Star-Gazette (Elmira, New York) 10 Dec 2002, Tue Page 10
Star-Gazette (Elmira, New York) 05 Nov 1961, Sun Page 16
Star-Gazette (Elmira, New York) 28 Sep 1966, Wed Page 12
https://www.livingplaces.com/NY/Chemung_County/Elmira_City/Maple_Avenue_Historic_District.html

REV. DR. AUGUSTUS WOODRUFF COWLES

Photograph taken on the occasion of his presentation of diplomas to the first graduating class, in 1859.

Image of Dr. Cowles, *Star-Gazette* May 29, 1930. Page 13

Augustus Cowles, The First President of Elmira Female College

by James Hare

In her novel, "Little Women," written in 1868, Louisa May Alcott wrote, "Women have minds and souls as well as hearts, and they've got ambition and talent as well as beauty. And I'm sick of people saying that love is all a woman is fit for. I'm sick of it...."

In his inaugural address, Dr. Augustus Cowles, as the first President of Elmira Female College, given in 1856 considered "the true mission of women." The word "Female" was dropped in 1890.

He stated, "There are doubtless some differences in relative proportion between the capabilities of the sexes as compared with each other. However, it is not plain whether this is inherent, or to be traced to physical causes and external circumstances. In pure intellection, in profound abstract thinking, any given number of females will probably be found somewhat inferior to men, both having the same advantages, while on the other hand, in the receptive and retentive powers—in apprehending imagery and in combining ideal forms—in the play of fancy and moral sensibilities women are undoubtedly superior...." It would appear that Cowles and Alcott if they met, might have a spirited debate.

Dr. Cowles served as president until 1889 when upon resignation, he was elected President Emeritus. He returned to fill in as acting president in 1896-97 while a new president was sought after. He died in March 1913, four months short of his 94th birthday on July 12, and now rests in Woodlawn Cemetery.

Cowles continues in his inaugural, "We are willing to look calmly, thoughtfully, prayerfully, upon the claims of the gentler, lovelier sex. We do most earnestly desire to secure our mothers, our wives, our daughters, names which nestle in our warmest affections all their rights and to redress all their wrongs." Eight years after the *Declaration of Sentiments* was proclaimed in Seneca Falls, New York, and indeed with the opening of Elmira College, the role of women in society was an issue.

Augustus Cowles was born on July 12, 1819, in the Town of Reading in Schuyler County, New York. He was the oldest of six children (four boys and two girls).

According to historian Ausburn Towner in *Our County and Its People,* he "began life with a diminutive body, which weighed at birth scarcely more than three pounds...He was so small that he gained special credit for precocity."

His mother taught him to read before he was five.

At age twelve, he studied Latin and Greek and was ready for Yale at sixteen, but was too young and did not have the money. His father obtained a position in a dry goods store for him, and he worked there for two years. In September 1838, he entered the sophomore class at Union College in Schenectady, New York. Using his artistic talents, he earned money enlarging illustrations for one of his professors and painted miniatures on ivory. Much of his study in College was in preparation for the ministry.

In 1841, he took charge of an academy in Schoharie County, New York. He taught French, Latin, Greek, higher algebra, geometry, chemistry, and "other subjects." He entered the Union Theological Seminary in 1843. Upon completing his seminary studies in 1846, he accepted the call to a Presbyterian Church in Brockport, New York. On June 15, 1847, Cowles married Frances Caroline Goold.They would have four children while in Brockport and two more born in Elmira. In his *Reminiscenses,* Cowles describes his introduction to Elmira:

"The way I came to know Elmira was a bit romantic. A ministerial friend of mine visited me in Brockport and preached for me. He was looking for a wife and was on his way to Geneva to see a daughter of Professor Boyd, who was the principal literary founder of Elmira College. He was an author employed by Harpers and had declined the presidency of Elmira College. My friend mentioned my name to him, and I soon received a letter from Professor Boyd, which opened our correspondence in the summer of 1855."

Cowles was elected to the presidency of the College in 1855, but when he went to the Presbytery, they voted to have him remain in the ministry at Brockport. At that point, Simeon Benjamin and the pastor of the First Presbyterian Church, Dr. David Murdock, asserted themselves. Dr. Murdock wrote to Cowles, making it clear now was the time to make a decision.

"I am as confident as I can be of anything, on which two opinions can be formed, that it is your Master calls you hither. The way seems as clear as it is possible to see anything in this uncertain life. It is all the more visible for the apprehension of duty the way has been gradually becoming clearer...I have advised Mr. Benjamin to get the Trustees to renew their application to you for it does seem that Providence points the finger to you and you alone at this time. If it was a "splendid risk" six months ago, the splendor is none the less, and the risk has diminished more than half."

At the time of Murdock's letter, the second session of the College had "160 boarders with 40 day students = 200." Finances had improved with a state appropriation, income from the students' fees, and Simeon Benjamin handling the debt.

Murdock concluded his letter by writing, "judgment if not followed (i.e., the call of God and man) has but one such chance in a lifetime." Cowles accepted and was inaugurated on August 7, 1856.

According to Towner, "besides presiding over the college, he has at times filled the chairs of Latin and Greek, and all the time those of mental and moral philosophy, Christian evidences, Biblical literature, and aesthetics."

Dr. Cowles clarified the mission of women as his inaugural speech

Ivy-clad Cowles Hall, Heart of College

Its turrets crowning majestic College Hill, historic Cowles Hall stands as a memorial to the character and works of the first president, for whom it is named.

Elmira College in its early days. *Star-Gazette* May 29, 1930. Page 13.

neared conclusion: "The mission of women demands thorough, judicious, well balanced and well-sustained culture of the taste and the intellect... Above all the mission of women requires true piety.

Her mission should be to make the world purer, holier, happier... The mission of this College is a holy one, it is a child of prayer: like its older sister Mt. Holyoke, religious plans and purposes lie at its foundations... We hope to do something to elevate the scholarship of the sex. We hope to promote the "rights of women" to a larger share of education. We design to furnish an institution where the most gifted and intellectual may pursue a course of thorough and extended study with all the advantages now enjoyed in our most favored Colleges, and we hope above all to maintain a highly cultivated religious influence."

Dr. Cowles was firmly on religious grounds in his role as president of Elmira College. He challenged "the world to produce any system which can be compared to the Bible for the elevation of women. With all its precepts of subjection and restrictions, the word of God is the *Magna Carta* of woman's rights...."

In a letter to Ezra Cornell on January 28, 1867, Cowles is perhaps most evident in his and the College's goal. He believed that the "five or six years before marriage are too often wasted in romance in society or useless though sometimes tasteful fancy work. In this most important period of a young woman's life, she too often becomes selfish, craving compliments and attention—silly and aimless-often yielding to the extremes of folly and extravagance. This is becoming a serious social defect in American society." He pointed out that, "the college was chartered in 1855, not with any radical notions of women's rights—or new professions or employments but simply to improve female education in the same proportion with the improved character of our Colleges and Universities...."

Nathaniel Ball, the Elmira College Archivist, has studied and spoken about Cowles. He has noted, "I believe that Cowles can't be viewed as a progressive through today's lens, but in total, Cowles spent fifty years

Today's McKinnon Park was once Hall's Swamp. As late as 1942, it was still a swamp and a public dumping ground. Elm Chevrolet purchased it with hopes for it to become an automobile garage. That never happened, and the land became McKinnon Park sometime around 1950. Photo by Diane Janowski.

So, Whose Alligator Was It? A Story with Five Versions

by Diane Janowski

I like stories with mystery. This story is a weird, twisted mystery story that got more bizarre over several days.

Urban legend has it that sometime around 1916, "a baby alligator got loose in Elmira." On May 20, 1919, the *Star-Gazette* got wind of a "sea-serpent" or "something" seen slithering on the bank of Newtown Creek. "It had a big mouth and scales." Maybe it was the missing alligator. Now, I must mention that in researching this legend, over four days with as many articles, the *Star-Gazette* sometimes called it an alligator, and sometimes a crocodile. I'll stick with "alligator" in this article.

Mothers in nearby Frog Hollow started guarding their children - and no more playing down by the creek, which is really hard if you live near a creek.

Version #1: On May 21, 1919, the *Star-Gazette* said the young James Grady, son of Mr. and Mrs. Michael Grady of 1319 Pratt Street, was a student at Elmira Free Academy. Three years prior, a friend of James' sent him a package. In the box was a tiny alligator about six inches in length. James loved the little fellow dearly, but somehow the alligator escaped. Where he went, James did not know.

It is believed that the alligator made its way to Hall's Swamp (today's McKinnon Park) and set up housekeeping. Supposedly, the reptile grew and prospered, and reached the size of six feet long. There was a drain in Hall's Swamp that led to Newtown Creek. During a high-water experience, the gator must have made his way into Newtown Creek were the surroundings were nicer, and the water was deeper.

Folks who lived along the creek reported hearing "peculiar noises" not typically made by the perch or muskrats in the area. Photographers were urged to go to the swamp and snap its photo for proof. To my knowledge, there are none.

Version #2: Later in the same article, the *Star-Gazette* reported that it was not an alligator but a crocodile. And, instead of the kid Grady, Humane Officer John Dilmore claimed an Elmira College faculty member placed the baby crocodile in the cold-water fountain in front of the courthouse to test its endurance. Elmira College denied that claim. Dilmore says that he retrieved the tiny gator but didn't explain its arrival to the swamp.

Version #3: The next day, Deputy Sheriff Lee Knapp came forward and claimed he put the gator in the Lake Street fountain. But he said it was a crocodile, not an alligator, and he was pretty sure the Hall's Swamp gator was his. Knapp claimed he gave the pet to George Helstrom, who lived in the vicinity of the swamp. Mr. Helstrom commented that he did have the alligator, and it did escape about three years earlier. Helstrom described it as three feet long at the time of the escape, and it had been strong enough to bite off a broom handle when poked. Helstrom said that crocodiles have "funnier noises" than alligators.

Version #4: Now, the story started to get clearer, or maybe muddier on the third day, May 23, 1919. Deputy Knapp now remembered that Harry Bach of Wellsburg gave him the alligator. The pet had come from the south and grew to three feet long. "With an idea of beautifying the courthouse lawn, Deputy Sherriff Knapp placed the gator in the pool of the fountain in front of the County Clerk's office. The reptile was admired by many until some kind-hearted person raised the question of cruelty to animals." It was thought that the cold water caused the animal suffering, so Humane Officer Dilmore acted. He contacted a biologist and sought expert advice.

The biologist said, "Yes, it was suffering in the cold water." So Dilmore gave it to Knapp, who gave it to Helstrom.

Next comes my question, "Whose alligator was it, the Grady kid's as in version 1, or Helstrom's as in version 3?" Inquiring minds need to know.

On May 24, a Star-Gazette report asked not if there was an alligator in Hall's Swamp, but how many alligators were there? One or two? Neighbors believed there was only one. The newspaper stories and neighborhood rumors had gotten out of hand.

"It had a big mouth and scales."

Version #5: Finally, we get to a partial conclusion. As it turned out, the kid James Grady, was Mr. Helstrom's nephew. The gator was not three-feet long at that time of its escape, but still a baby. And the Helstrom gator was given to young nephew James as a pet. James, being busy with school and all, was not the best caregiver, and the gator took his chances on the run. It ran right down the street to the nearest swamp. Mr. Gator, eventually, did become six feet long on his own. It spent two summers and winters on his own in the swamp. James forgot about his pet. Neighbors thought there was a "sick goose in the swamp," but after several sightings of the reptile, they knew what the funny noise was.

"There is a danger for the children of the vicinity, and for this reason, parents are suffering anxiety." Neighbors with cameras went looking with no avail.

This story doesn't have an ending, or at least I was unable to find it. Mr. Gator was never caught.

What is the life expectancy of alligators in New York?

Sources:

Star-Gazette (Elmira, New York) May 21, 1919, Wed Page 4
Star-Gazette(Elmira, New York) May 22, 1919, Thu Page 7
Star-Gazette (Elmira, New York)May 22, 1919, Thu Page 14
Star-Gazette (Elmira, New York) May 23, 1919, Fri Page 7

Elmira's Foremost Citizen

by James Hare

In 1886, Edward J. Dunn was offered a position as bookkeeper in the Chemung Canal Bank at $25 per month. He was promoted from time to time and in 1901 was elected assistant cashier. When the Chemung Canal Trust Company was formed in 1903, Dunn was elected treasurer.

Image from the *Star-Gazette* (Elmira, New York) 04 Jul 1976, Page 86

In 1919, he assumed the duties of the president, serving until his resignation in 1925. According to his obituary in the *Star-Gazette* on October 24, 1927, "The terms under which Mr. Dunn accepted the position of president of this institution were typical of his conception of the fitness of things for he stipulated that his services in this connection be given without compensation."

Edward J. Dunn, at his death, was recognized as "Elmira's foremost citizen." He was president of the Eclipse Machine Company of Elmira; The Eclipse Machine Company Limited of Walkersville, Ontario, Canada; The Eclipse Textile Devices Inc. of Elmira; The Dunn

Realty Corporation and Dunn-Cooper Corporation both of Elmira; executor of the Mathias H. Arnot Estate of Elmira; a director of the Elmira, Water, Light, and Railroad Company, the Shepard Electric Crane-Hoist Company of Montour Falls, the Johnson Oil Refining Company of Chicago, the American La France Fire Engine Company, Elmira Knitting Mills and director and past president of the Elmira Association of Commerce. Dunn was also a trustee of the Chemung County Historical Society, Past President of the Arctic League, Vice President of the Elmira Council of Boy Scouts, a Vice President of the Arnot Art Gallery, an Elk, a Knight of Columbus, a member of Rotary, the City Club, Century Club, and the Golf and Country Club. During World War I, he was the executive chair of eight counties on the War Industries Committee.

Edward J. Dunn was born to Patrick and Bridgett O'Brien Dunn on January 23, 1868, at 166 DeWitt Avenue.

He was baptized a few weeks later at St. Peter and Paul's Church. Edward attended public schools and graduated from Elmira Free Academy. His older brother, William, was ordained a priest, and according to Catharine Connelly, in her March 1964 article in the Chemung County *Historical Journal,* he emphasized to his younger brother, "the Biblical philosophy of stewardship and brotherly love."

Edward's obituary attests to how well he understood those lessons.

> *"Thousands of dollars of the fortune he had amassed were distributed without publicity to untold numbers of worthy charities to assist unfortunate families who had tasted the cup of adversity, and to struggling boys and girls desirous of obtaining an education, but without the means to that end. Never did the question of class, race, or creed interfere with the man's generosity...."*

"Dunn was a vital lifesaver of sorts for St. Joseph's Hospital in times when the founding nuns encountered financial problems."

Dunn's integrity and business acumen were shown when he met Vincent Bendix. Bendix had designed the Bendix Motor Buggy between 1907 and 1909 and started an automobile firm. Seven thousand buggies later, he went bankrupt. In 1913, Dunn was managing the Eclipse Machine Company, manufacturing coaster brakes for bicycles, pulleys, and other devices. The Eclipse Company had a booth at the National Motorcycle and Bicycle Show in Chicago. Bendix appeared a the booth, and after a lengthy discussion with the attendant produced from his bag"a queer-looking device, an invention of his own which he declared would start an automobile by the mere pressure of a button and which if properly exploited, would relegate all hand-cranked motor cars to the scrap heap." (*Star-Gazette* obituary October 24, 1927) The Eclipse man suggested that Bendix meet Mr. Dunn the next day. They met, they talked, they shook hands. Two months later, they signed a handwritten agreement drafted by Dunn.

The Bendix Drive was born and brought prosperity to the Eclipse Company and the Elmira Community.

One of the lasting memorials to Dunn is Dunn Field. The stadium, as we know it, was built after his passing, but if not for him, Elmira might not have such a facility. Baseball began in the late 1800s and was initially played in the Maple Avenue Driving Park. Eventually, this became Recreation Park, and a new stadium was built in 1914 and was Elmira's principal baseball grounds. In 1919-1920 the park

Dunn Field became a reality after Edward J. Dunn gave Elmira the land for the facility.

Image from the *Star-Gazette* (Elmira, New York) 04 Jul 1976, Page 86

was being dismantled. The grandstand had been sold, and the disposal of the park's equipment was underway. In 1920 Dunn purchased the property, transferring its management to the Dunn Field Corporation, with the net income being given to charity. It assured the city of a permanent baseball center for both professional and amateur organizations. The property was eventually deeded to Elmira. When the stadium burned down in 1938, the new stadium, built in 1939, was named Dunn Field.

Forty years after Dunn's birth on DeWitt Avenue, St. Joseph's Hospital opened, "a stone's throw" from his family home. His support for the hospital would be real evidence that his brother's guidance was instilled in his character. On October 30, 1927, the *Sunday Telegram* noted that "Dunn was a vital lifesaver of sorts for St. Joseph's Hospital in times when the founding nuns encountered financial problems."

In 1919, he headed a drive that raised $300,000 of public funds, including substantial sums of his own to erect a badly needed surgical building. The benefactor then assumed payment of interest on the building mortgage until the debt paid off through a city-wide appeal in 1927.

When it was discovered that the Dunn will left one million dollars ($14,193,954 in 2019 dollars) to the hospital, plans were drawn up for a nurse's residence, which also would serve as a training center for student nurses.

Therein was born Dunn Memorial, the imposing building on De Witt Avenue...."

On the day of his funeral, the community witnessed an unusual tribute. The *Telegram* reported that. "During the funeral at St. Patrick's Church, a plane circled the Northside church in a huge spiral. When the procession left the church...for St. Peter and Paul's Cemetery, the low flying craft led the procession.

At the close of the ceremony at the grave, flowers were dropped from the plane, scattering around his resting place.

The tribute resulted from Dunn's interest in aviation and the assistance he gave Daniel and Floyd Hungerford, pioneers in airplane building and flying in Elmira.

Dunn provided them an airport that served as the base of the Elmira Airplane Exhibition Corporation. He often gave the Hungerfords advice on business dealings. In gratitude, they gave a final salute from the air."

A Pudgie's ad in the *Star-Gazette* dated March 9, 1967

Yankee Doodle Pizza at the Pioneer Restaurant in the *Star-Gazette*, December 21, 1954.

Love at First Slice

by Diane Janowski

I asked my Facebook people on "ChemungHistory.com" about pizza, and as a group, we came up with 63 local pizza places in our collective memory. In researching pizzerias around Elmira, I found the first occurrence of the word "pizza" used as a food, not as a last name, on January 9, 1935, in the *Star-Gazette*. In a column called "Sister Mary's Kitchen," a dinner menu that included "pizza Neapolitan." The article said that it was invented in Manhattan and was a pastry of sorts. Ingredients included an onion, butter, one tomato, minced mushrooms, grated Swiss cheese, one egg, mixed herbs, salt, and pepper. Oh, and a pie crust.

By 1944 the world was getting more sophisticated. An article titled "Hi Ya, Stranger" by Dorothy Kilgallen recommended a restaurant in Manhattan called Marconi's Restaurant and Pizzeria. She said a "pizza pie" is the "size of an average night club table for two, and made of dough, tomato sauce, and a special Italian cheese."

November 6, 1944, saw Elmira's first real pizzeria - Mike's Restaurant at 422 East Water Street – across from today's Chemung County Historical Society.

The second pizza restaurant started serving "Hot Italian Pie" was Clate's Homestead Tavern at the point in West Elmira in December 1945. Also, on the menu was gnocchi, veal scallopini, chicken a la cacciatore, bracciole, and spaghetti with tuna fish sauce.

1946 and we get Mustico's. They claimed to be Elmira's only real pizzeria. Their new delicious creation, "La Pizza" came with the slogan "Watch this Italian pie made and baked in a few minutes." Mustico's was at the corner of North Main and Bloomer Avenue.

On July 10, 1947, Dorothy Kilgallen's syndicated column again mentioned the joys of pizza, this time at Coney Island, where "pizza pies were bigger than the moon."

On August 4, 1947, Elmira's Moretti's restaurant on Hatch Street began serving Italian pizza.

Liberatore's Grille on West Fifth served pizza in 1948. In 1948, the Imperial Hotel on West First Street served "Real Italian Pizza (Tomato Pie). Choices for toppings included none, anchovies, cheese, mushroom, tuna fish, and green peppers. Luckily this tuna fish idea did not last long.

In 1949, "La Pizza" was served at the Pioneer Restaurant at 210 South Main Street. The Pioneer also had an accordion player on Mondays and Wednesdays. In November 1949, their pizza came with "Muzzarella" cheese, and you could have either the new Brooklyn style or regular.

In 1951 the Hellmann's company ran a recipe advertisement for their version of homemade Pizza Pies. All you needed was Hellmann's mayonnaise, English muffin halves, tomato slices, anchovy fillets, and parmesan cheese. "Broil until mayonnaise is brown." Sounds easy enough. Who doesn't love browned mayonnaise?

The Appian Way company sold a pre-packaged pizza mix that was first advertised in 1952 at the Elmira Market Place supermarket in Langdon Plaza. "Make your own for only 55¢."

In the 1950s, Elmira saw the Center Restaurant in the Southport Shopping Center serving "Pizza Napolitaine." "Hot Pizza Pie" was served at the Palms on North Main Street. Sam's Grill at 304 East Washington Avenue started serving pizza in 1952. In 1953 a new pizza oven was installed at the Pioneer. It would double their production. In 1953, Coppola's Restaurant, opposite Remington-Rand, claimed to serve the "best pizza."

Restaurants tried to outdo each other. In 1954, Arcadi's Restaurant at 109 East McCann's Boulevard, went all out with two choices in pizza – plain tomato or tomato and cheese. In 1954 the Pioneer started an ordering service for "pan-cut and ready to serve" for parties and showers.

Again, not to be outdone, the Pioneer went an extra step in November 1954 – with their "Yankee Doodle Pizza" with beans. Because of the name, I am thinking of baked beans, but you can use your imagination with that.

In 1955, Masia's in Pine City got in on the pizza deal. They bought themselves a pizza oven. Their choices in toppings included meat sauce, anchovies, pepperoni, mushrooms, Polish sausage, Italian sausage, or any combination. Also, that year, the Spaghetti Palace on the Miracle Mile started serving pizza.

Wellsburg's Village Tavern got on the ball in 1961. Super Duper supermarket started selling frozen pizzas targeted to the teenage audience with a good deal - 3 for 99¢. Danna's and Zarro's opened in the 1960s.

Now in 1963 came Pudgie's at 528 North Main Street and in 1967 on Mt. Zoar Street. The north side location claimed it was the first exclusively pizza restaurant with 14 varieties because "most everyone likes pizza." And they offered delivery! But they were closed on Mondays. Within two years, they had outgrown their facility and remodeled the whole operation, making them the "King of the Pizzas." They enlarged their staff and upgraded the selection to 21 toppings. In 1967 also came Pudgie's 32-slice sheet pizza – "a hit at any party." By 1971 Pudgie's boasted 52 different toppings. The South Main Street location opened in 1976.

In the 1960s, our area exploded with Robbie's Pizza, Park View Tavern, Danna's, Rohan's Deli, Pasquale's (not to be confused with a later pizza restaurant also named Pasquale's) Cavaluzzi's, and Speedy's (changed to Mr. Speedy's soon after). In the 1970s came Denny's, Chef Italia and Leo's Tavern, and The Pizza Pit. Chain restaurant Pizza Hut on the Miracle Mile opened in 1973. The Pizza Hut on Broadway and Pizza World opened in 1976, and downtown Elmira got its own Pizza Hut in 1984. Picnic Pizza originated in Brooklyn, of course. It got its start at the Arnot Mall in 1980. Then came Hawk's Pizza, Bernie Murray's, Campus Pizza, Pizza Pick-Up, and Enrico's. The 1990s brought us Gino's, Papa G's, Gaetano's, Rico's – not to be confused with Enrico's), Pietro and Sons, Charlie C.'s, Buck's Pizza, and Vincenzo's. Original Italian Pizza first arrived in 1994 and came back in 2000. The 2000s brought us Paesano's, Tanino's, Louie's, Nirchi's, Jerlando's, and Guiseppe's.

And that's mostly it for the local history of pizza. I didn't mention the chains Little Caesars, Papa John's, and Domino's that have come and gone - and come back and moved around several times.

In 75 years of local pizza places, Elmirans have eaten thousands, or maybe millions of slices. Today when I asked Siri about pizza, she says Elmira has 21 places serving pizza. Go get yourself a slice.

Sources:

Star-Gazette (Elmira, New York) September 22, 1944, Fri Page 6
Star-Gazette (Elmira, New York) April 11, 1952, Fri Page 13
Star-Gazette (Elmira, New York) May 10, 1953, Sun Page 43
Star-Gazette (Elmira, New York) November 13, 1954, Sat Page 9
Star-Gazette (Elmira, New York) March 4, 1961, Sat Page 9
Star-Gazette (Elmira, New York) March 9, 1967, Thu Page 16

A'don Allen and Bessie Berry. Image from *Star-Gazette* (Elmira, New York)23 Feb 2020, Page A2

A'don Allen and Bessie Berry

by James Hare

In the November 1993 election for the Elmira City Council, the 5-2 Democratic majority was replaced with a 5-2 Republican majority. Deputy Mayor and Second District Councilman A'Don Allen was one of the two Democrats who survived the election. On election night, a young news reporter asked Allen what it felt like to be in the minority?

Allen, aged 77, and the first African American, and at that time, the only African American elected to the council, responded, "I've been a minority all my life, I think I can handle it."

In the Elmira City School Board election in 1966, Mrs. Bessie Berry was elected. The *Star-Gazette* reported on May 4, 1966, that Mrs. Berry is not the first woman on the board, but she is the first Negro (sic) on the board." Berry said, "being a first doesn't faze me at all, I suppose I was the first in Child Welfare. I don't think of it one way or another."

Both Allen and Berry accumulated "firsts" in their service to the Elmira community. Allen was the first African American appointed to the Elmira Civil Service Commission in 1968. In 1969, he made political history when he was elected 4th Ward Supervisor and became the first African American member of the Chemung County Board of Supervisors (now the County Legislature). In 1977, he became the first African American elected to the Elmira City Council. He was elected nine times to that position. I had the honor as Mayor in 1988, to ask A'Don to become Deputy Mayor.

When appointed in 1967, Bessie Berry became the first African American social worker and probation officer in Chemung County.

In 1981, she became the first African American Corrections Counselor at the Elmira Correctional Facility.

Outside that significant professional career, Bessie was the first African American elected to the Elmira School District Board of Education in 1966, where she would serve two five year terms.

A'Don Allen was born May 1, 1916, in Dillon, South Carolina. He was the only son of Henry and Laura Allen. The family moved to Elmira in 1924 when A'Don was eight years old.

He once told me that he remembered the Ku Klux Klan parade of 1925 in Elmira. Allen attended Elmira Free Academy and played basketball for EFA in the early 1930s. At his passing in 1993, the late Charlie Bright, a civic leader in his own right, recalled that the "two of them were friends and competitors from different sides of the river and would often meet at the former Neighborhood House where they would settle disputes. We were competitive...he was a little more competitive than I was because he was always bigger than I was." During World War II, Allen served 33 months in the Pacific, winning a Bronze Star as a member of the Army Corps of Engineers at Okinawa.

Returning from the war, he worked many jobs finally selected a career as a barber opening his shop on the Eastside.

He married Lillian Dunham in 1955. They would have two children, Carol and A'Don Allen Jr.

Allen was a very active member of the Monumental Baptist Church, chairing the trustees' board for many years. In 1967, the NAACP gave him an award for bringing in 100 memberships. He was also a 33rd degree Mason and member of the Mt. Nebo Lodge No. 8 here in Elmira. In July of 1964, he was appointed the district deputy grand master of the Sixth Masonic District, which covered much of central New York.

Bessie Thompson Berry was born September 6, 1931, and raised in Memphis, Tennessee. She was the youngest child of Benjamin and Gertrude Sanders Thompson. After attending high school in Memphis, she went to Tennessee State A&I University in Nashville. While in school, she met Theodore F. Berry Jr. from Elmira. They were married in 1953 and, upon graduation, moved to Elmira. The Berrys had two children, Theodore F. Berry III and Carmela. The Berrys lived on the Eastside when they first settled in the city. She served faithfully and actively in the Frederick Douglas Memorial A.M.E. Zion Church as secretary and pianist. She also worked with the church youth as a counselor and advocate.

In 1956 Berry sought part-time work at the New York State Employment Office. She worked short term at several sites and was assigned to the Chemung County Probation Department doing secretarial work.

Eventually, she took a civil service exam and was appointed a probation officer in 1967. She was a county employee until 1981 when she became a corrections counselor at the Elmira Correctional Facility.

In an interview conducted by Joann Browne, on file at the Chemung County Historical Society, Berry was asked whether "being black caused her any difficulty getting a job?" Berry responded, "At that time, I personally had not had problems getting any of the jobs that I had applied for except the job at the Elmira Correctional Facility.

Berry was acting President of the local NAACP Chapter in 1984 and elected President in 1985, serving until 1988. County Legislator Marty Chalk recalls that he served with Berry on the original Board of Directors for the Ernie Davis Community Center. He commented that after every meeting, Bessie would tell him to "keep the faith."

As councilman A'Don Allen attacked the issues that impacted his district and, indeed, the city. He used his energy to combat the drug problem, deterioration of neighborhoods, and supported the development of the Ernie Davis Community Center. The new East Avenue Bridge was completed while he was in office, and he was a leader in developing programs such as rental rehabilitation, paint up, fix up and the former dumpster neighborhood cleanup.

A'Don was a quiet man; I am loquacious. As my deputy mayor, he often quipped that he liked speaking after the Mayor because there was not much left to say. But we felt he was like E. F. Hutton; when he spoke, everyone listened.

Bessie Berry was much more outspoken. She was passionate about the causes she believed in. Having been elected to the school board in 1966, she was on the board when Dr. Martin Luther King Jr. was assassinated. Bessie would be a leader in the fight. Indeed it was a fight to have January 15 declared a holiday in his honor. In March 1970, the Chemung County Human Relations Commission passed two resolutions on the issue. One was sent to the state and national representatives urging a national holiday, and the other to local Chemung County School Boards urging them to declare a holiday.

Berry introduced a resolution to the Elmira City School Board at the May 12th meeting to make January 15 a permanent holiday. Her resolution was defeated; she walked out. Her motion was immediately followed by a motion to make the holiday for one year, with Berry not voting. When contacted later, she was quoted in the May 13, 1970, *Star-Gazette* saying, "It makes no difference to me. I certainly would have voted that down. We're so accustomed to tests. We have to prove ourselves. Why?"

The reason for her objection was that many did not want a holiday; they wanted just a day of study and discussion. She contrasted that with Columbus Day, Labor Day, President's birthdays, and asked why.

Issues arose with the teacher's union, and indeed a resolution before the Chemung County Board of Supervisors failed.

Mrs. Berry would eventually succeed in getting the district to adopt the holiday yearly until it became a national holiday.

Once again, she raised her voice, this time to the Human Relations Commission. In the *Star-Gazette* of May 12, 1971, she challenged them saying, "...you should go out and get off your duffs and secure a holiday for Chemung County."

It has been claimed that the Elmira City School District was the first community in the state to declare January 15 as a holiday in honor of Dr. Martin Luther King Jr. It appears that a school district in the Town of Greenborough in Westchester County and another in New York City may have preceded Elmira, but if not the first, we were among the first in the effort, and Bessie Berry led the charge.

The efforts of A'Don Allen and Bessie Berry, aided by many others, brought our community to a better place. Their strength and persistence, and indeed courage are an example for others to follow.

RATHBUN DINNERS.

Specialties for to-morrow's dinner at the Hotel Rathbun will be Terrapin soup, chicken halibut, soft shell crabs, lamb fries, New York spring lamb, smothered squab, strawberry short cake, new asparagus, new wax beans, new peas and all the other new vegetables in the market.

Image from the *Star-Gazette* (Elmira, New York) 13 May 1899, Page 5.

Elegant Elmira

by Diane Janowski

Elmirans used to eat more elegantly than today. J. D. Iles asked me last month what kinds of foods Samuel Clemens (our Mark Twain) used to eat. That got me thinking. When Sam was in Elmira, he stayed with either his in-laws on North Main Street or his sister-in-law's Susan Crane's house (Quarry Farm). So, what was served? And when he went downtown to the two big restaurants, what did he order?

As far as eating at Quarry Farm, Susan Crane much preferred Miss Maria Parloa's New Cook Book, printed in 1880. Miss Parloa was much like today's Chef Gordon Ramsay – a celebrity chef. Her books were in everyone's home. Hotel restaurants modeled their menus after her recipes as well.

On July 18, 1891, Mr. Maxwell Haight, owner of the Rathbun House, Elmira's premier hotel, served a banquet to the Elmira Board of Trade in his dining room. On the buffet table were Little Neck Clams, Imperial sherry, Green Turtle Soup, Boiled Halibut with Caper Sauce, Olives, Potatoes in Cream, Broiled Spring Chicken, French Fried Potatoes, French Peas, *St. Estephe*, Filet of Beef with Mushroom Sauce, Butter Beans, Asparagus, Lobster Salad, Potato Salad, wafer crackers, Roman punch, Squab on toast, Saratoga Potatoes, Neapolitan ice cream, Mumm's, Roquefort cheese, toasted crackers, Coffee, and Cigars. Now that is a buffet. I know French fries. I had to google *St. Estephe* – it is a wine from the Bordeaux region. "Roman Punch," a famous cocktail of the 1800s, is a combination of citrus juice, champagne and rum, sugar, and frothy meringue on top. Yes, this was in downtown Elmira. Saratoga potatoes are now known as potato chips.

On April 26, 1892, Miss Fannie Strauss married Maurice Garson at the High Street Temple. After the ceremony, the 100 guests were driven in carriages to the Rathbun Hotel. Their dinner included Imperial Sherry, Blue Points on Shell, *Purée a la Reine*, Kennebeck Salmon with Hollandaise, Boiled New Potatoes, Queen Olives, Sweet Bread Patties *Toulouse*, Tenderloin of Beef with Mushrooms, Kempner Berg, Lobster Salad, Broiled Spring Chicken, Benedictine, French Peas, Stuffed Philadelphia Squab, French Fried Potatoes, Moët and Chandon, Strawberries with cream. *Café Noir* and assorted cakes.

On May 17, 1897, at the Langwell Hotel on State Street, a group of local physicians held their annual Medical Society met to hear Dr. C. A. Murray's paper "Blood Letting" followed by a sumptuous banquet of Terrapin Soup, Boiled Chicken, Halibut with Shrimp Sauce, *Parisienne* Potatoes, Great Western [wine], Roasted Canvas-Back Ducks, New Browned Potatoes, Punch *a la Reine*, Broiled Lamb Chops, New Peas, Fresh Lobster Salad with Mayonnaise Dressing, Strawberry Shortcake with whipped cream, Walnut Layer Cake, Black coffee. I'm guessing that *Parisienne* potatoes are French fries.

On the evening of June 22, 1899, the Elmira Free Academy graduating class of 1899 held their banquet at the Langwell Hotel. On their menu was Little Neck Clams, New Lettuce, Sliced Potatoes, *Consommé Royale*, Baked Bluefish, Robert Sauce, "Roast Spring Lamb '99 with Green Mint Sauce," New String Beans, New Bermuda Potatoes with Cream Sauce, Lemon Water Ice, Soft Shell Crabs on Toast, Asparagus, Braised Sweetbreads with New Peas, Fresh Lobster Salad with Mayonnaise, Neapolitan Ice cream, American Cheese, *Café Noir*. Yes, high-schoolers were served this menu.

Elmira's City Club served *trés élegant* food also. On the evening of July 13, 1900, a reception for Spencer Meade, superintendent of the Northern Central Railroad, who was leaving Elmira to take a job in Philadelphia taking charge of the Pennsylvania Railroad. They gave Spencer a proper send-off with 75 in attendance. Manager Gus Kuhn "was

CLASS DAY.

An Enjoyable Time Held at the Langwell.

The class of '99 of the Elmira Free academy held their class day exercises and banquet at the Hotel Langwell last evening. The dining room and tables were beautifully decorated. De Waters' orchestra rendered inspiring music during the banquet. Toasts and impromptu remarks were given by several members of the class, and also by Professor Evans, Miss Mary K. Smith, and Miss Louise M. Godfrey. The program of the class day exercises as published in this paper last evening was carried out with the exception of the toast by Henry B. Reynolds, and proved very enjoyable. The menu which was served was as follows:

Little Neck Clams.
New Lettuce New Sliced Potatoes
Consomme Royale
Baked Bluefish, Robert Sauce.
Dolphine Potatoes.
Roast Spring Lamb '99, Green Mint Sauce.
New String Beans
New Bermuda Potatoes, Cream Sauce
Lemon Water Ice.
Soft Shell Crabs on Toast
Asparagus
Braised Sweetbreads with New Peas
Fresh Lobster Salad, Mayonaise Dressing
Neapolitan Ice Cream
Assorted Cake.
American Cheese Wafers
Cafe Noir

Graduation dinner for Elmira Free Academy Class of 1899, at the Langwell Hotel on June 23, 1899. *Star-Gazette.*

in charge of the spread, and the service and cooking were perfect." It was a delicious dinner, and Kuhn received many compliments. His menu included Champagne Punch, Anchovies on Toast, Mumm's Extra Dry, *Consommé* City Club, Salted Pecans, Salted Almonds, Kennebeck Salmon with Sauce Hollandaise, Cucumbers with French Dressing, Sweet Bread Croquettes, Tomato Salad with Mayonnaise, Roquefort and Brie cheese, and Coffee. "The reception lasted until late in the evening. Friendships were renewed, toasts were drunk, and it was an evening of rare enjoyment."

Now the Elmira Country Club dinner menu was harder to find. In fact, I didn't. The *Star-Gazette* reported that on June 3, 1906, an "elaborate dinner was served after the [golf] match. Levi Holmes, the new club steward from New York City, had charge of the culinary arrangements, and a most elaborate repast was provided. Many colored waiters had been engaged from the city to serve, but owning to difficulties and the steward and the waiters, they went on strike, and prompt service was handicapped in consequence."

Elmirans still enjoy buffet or banquet dinners. Many restaurants and hotels serve them on special occasions.

Sources:

Star-Gazette (Elmira, New York) June 19, 1891, Fri Page 5
Star-Gazette (Elmira, New York) May 26, 1906, Sat Page 5
Star-Gazette (Elmira, New York) August 15, 1965, Sun Page 11

The Founding of Trinity Episcopal Church

by James Hare

Benjamin Treadwell Onderdonk (1791-1861) Wikipedia public domain image.

In the early 1830s, a small "society" of Episcopalians had formed in the Village of Elmira. The Rt. Rev. B. T. Onderdonk, D. D., Bishop of the Diocese of New York, came to the village and conducted the first service of any record according to the *Trinity Church History* published in 1983.

Ausburn Towner, in his 1892 *History of Chemung County*, noted that the "society" was a mere handful at first.

He wrote "that some of those upon whose shoulders fell the early burdens of the church are remembered with a feeling of almost reverence...and one who by a kind-heartedness and never-disturbed good humor, acquired the name of Auntie Hill was instant and constant in her labors for the church." She and her husband, "Tommy" had come from Ireland in the 1820s. She is credited with circulating the first subscription paper for funding a church. The Trinity Church History notes that the church owes its beginning to her "more than to any other."

Following Bishop Onderdonk's visit, services were again held in Elmira in 1833, conducted by the Rev. James D. Carder, Missionary at Ithaca. A Sunday *Telegram* article from September 3, 1922, notes that "his coming was more or less of an event in the village, his robes and prayer book being a part of a religious service to which the neighborhood had never been accustomed...."

Trinity Church, Elmira, New York, 2008
Photographer: Lvklock. Wikipedia creative commons.

In a report given to the 1833 New York Diocesan Convention, Carder stated, "In Elmira...he performed divine service several times previous to the middle of July, and on June 12, 1833, organized a parish by the name Trinity Church."

He reported that at communion, "thirteen communicated, and one was repelled. In that year, three children were baptized, and there was one marriage."

The first rector was the Rev. Thomas Clark. He reported to the 1833 Convention, "I arrived in Elmira as Missionary...and found a small but zealous company of Episcopalians...some of them had lived without the services of the church for several years...I have commenced preaching in the District School Room, which I generally I have nearly full...." The *Telegram* described the schoolhouse, located where the Park Church now stands, "It was a bare, wild and cheerless place. The schoolmaster's table, on a low platform, served as a lectern, pulpit, and communion table. The wooden benches were hacked and hewn by the boys, and many a pane of glass was lacking from the eight windows." According to the writer, at the service held on Christmas Eve, 1833, the school was decorated, the room was full, with Colonel John Hendy standing in the doorway, "from curiosity as he was not much of a churchgoer."

At that service, it was announced that a subscription of $800 had been made by Trinity Church of New York City towards a new church in which to worship. It was generally understood that Auntie Hill had secured the donation on a recent trip to the city. In addition to the pledge, loads of stone for the foundation, a quantity of suitable lumber, window glass, and a donation by Abram Riker of a specified number of days for carpenter work were obtained. The new church was built on the corner of Railroad Avenue and Church Street at a cost of $3,150. Bishop Onderdonk officiated at the Service of Consecrated it on August 27, 1837.

The growth of the congregation would lead to the need for a larger building. In 1850, under the leadership of rector, the Rev. Andrew D. Hull, D.D. (1849-1866), the lot at the northeast corner of Main and Church Streets was purchased. A rectory was built in 1852. The services of architect Henry C. Dudley were obtained. He was renowned for church architecture in the Gothic Revival style, with his trademark being spires of the same material as the building. The cornerstone was laid on July 26, 1855. Trinity has a steeple (consisting of a tower and spire), which is of the same brick construction as the church. David England writes in the "History of Church Steeples" that we must consider the "spiritual function" of the steeple. "We are admonished by Christ, who said in *John 12:32*...And I, if I am lifted up from the earth (I), will draw all men unto me. While signifying what death he would die, this scripture also challenges us to lift the cross of Christ up to the world. When we see a steeple and cross atop a church pointing gracefully toward Heaven, the church is also lifting Christ up so that all men might be drawn to him and his promise."

Sitting atop the Trinity Steeple is a six-foot gold leaf cross. The steeple made of the same brick as the church is one of eleven of its kind in the world and seven of its kind in this country and according to the New York State Historic Preservation Office, the only one in the state. In 2007, Trinity Episcopal Church was added to the National Register of Historic Places.

Before construction was completed, Thomas Stewart and Ann Johnson became the first to be married in the new building. Stewart was a fugitive slave, a lesser-known, though no less loved and respected contemporary and friend of John W. Jones." He had made his way to Elmira via the Underground Railroad in 1853 and had been given a haven by the church. He was baptized on July 23, 1854, and confirmed on July 30.

On September 15, 1858, he and Ann were married after "walking up into the chancel on boards instead of steps."

...with Colonel John Hendy standing in the doorway, "from curiosity as he was not much of a churchgoer."

That year Stewart became Sexton of the church and served for forty years in that position.

The first service in the present Trinity Church building was held on July 4, 1858. The cost of construction was $30,000. Eight years later, on April 5, 1866, the church was consecrated after the debt had been paid. According to the April 6 *Daily Advertiser,*

> *"The solemn and impressive service of consecration took place... The Holy Bible, Book of Common Prayer and Communion vessels being bestowed to their places, the Rt. Rev. A. Cleveland Coxe D. D. Bishop of the Diocese (of Western New York, created in 1839) proceeded with appropriate prayers, and the Sentence of Consecration was read by the Rev. Mr. Parke of Waterloo and laid upon the altar."*

Update: Trinity Episcopal Church held its last service in September 2020.

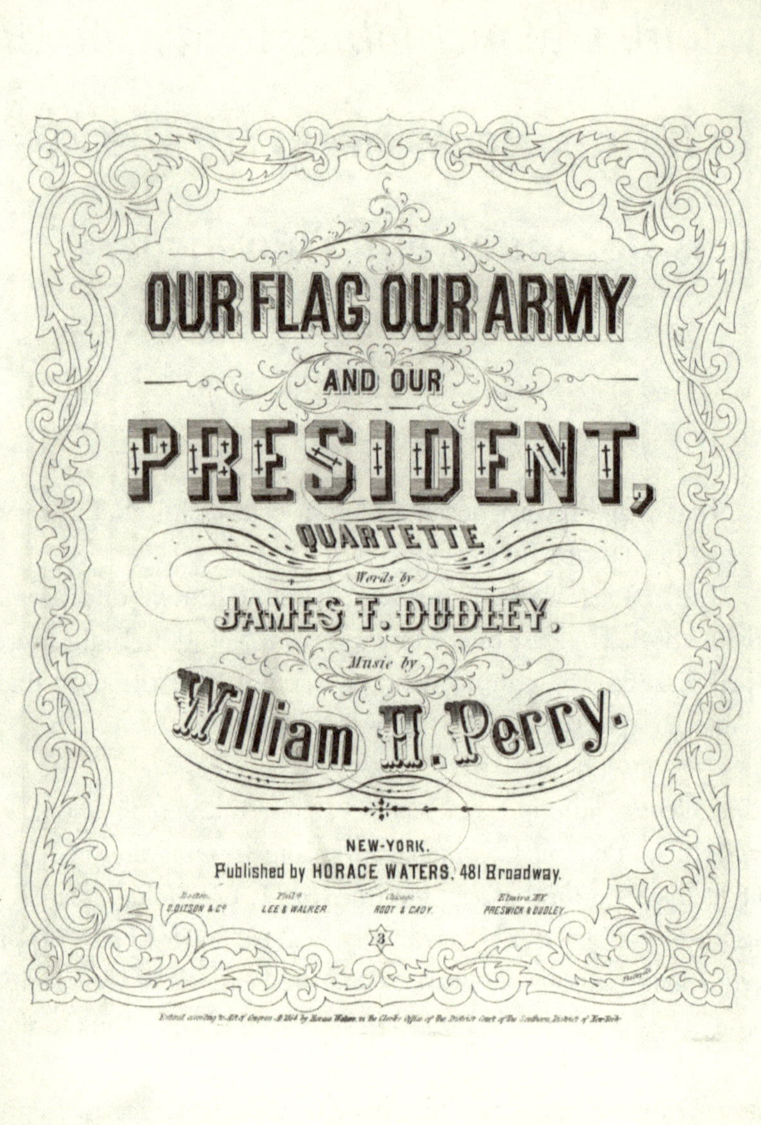

Perry, William H, and James T Dudley. Our flag, our army, and our president: quartette words by James T. Dudley; music by William H. Perry. Horace Waters, New York, 1864. Notated Music. https://www.loc.gov/item/scsm000135/."

December 1864 in Elmira

by Diane Janowski

In the holiday season of 1864, what was happening? From the Elmira *Daily Advertiser.*

On December 1 we learned how to make Yorkshire Pie. First, we need a large receptacle the size of a good cheese-box. Then complete with thick pie crust, a fine mellow Yorkshire ham if you can find one, or instead use a turkey, goose, several pheasant chickens, a hare. Next, we need a few slices of venison, half a dozen pigeons, 3 pounds of sausage, and herbs. Fill up the receptacle, add the top layer of crust. Bake in a cool oven for three or four hours. "Take out very gently and let stand until the next day." It will be a "bonnie big pie, too, but there is no fear of its spoiling for it will keep a couple of months."

Lincoln was still alive, and the war continued in the South. New sheet music titled "Our Flag, Our Army, Our President" was available at the Preswick & Dudley paper goods store at 114 Water Street.

At the Temple of Fashion at 139 Water Street, beaver coats were on sale. And not just any beavers – we had choices of All Wool Castor Beaver, Moscow Beavers, or Esquimaux Beavers.

On December 2 we learned that the Confederate prisoners were receiving "good treatment" while in Elmira. Apparently, "they eat 25% more than regular un-detained people. Bread is plentiful, and the soups look rich and savory."

On December 7, "Sherman's March through Georgia" continued. The Buckley & Crowle oyster shop on the corner of Lake and Carroll Streets sold "superior oysters" in cans, kegs, by the quart or gallon.

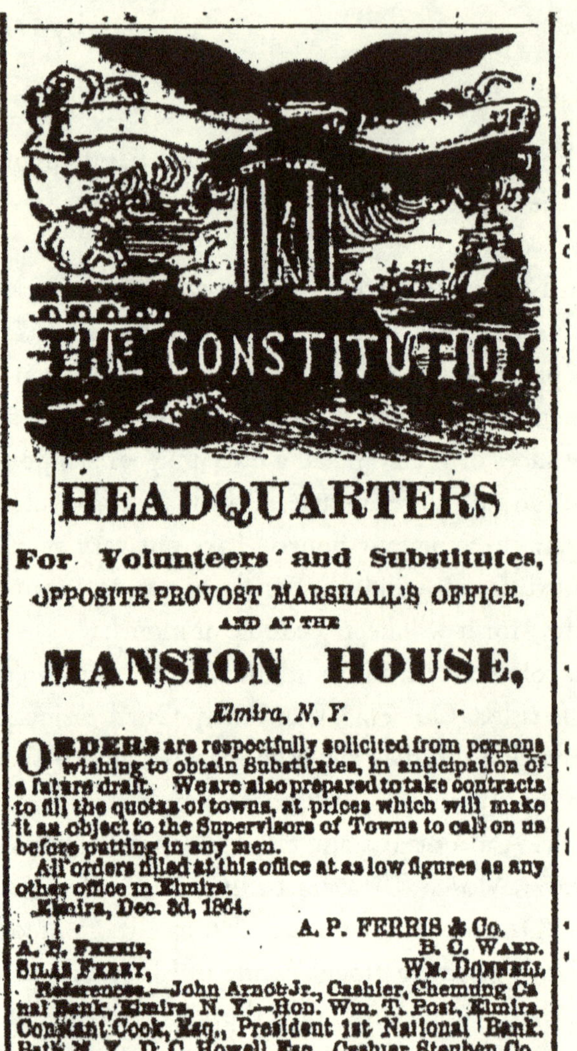

THE CONSTITUTION

HEADQUARTERS

For Volunteers and Substitutes,

OPPOSITE PROVOST MARSHALL'S OFFICE,

AND AT THE

MANSION HOUSE,

Elmira, N. Y.

ORDERS are respectfully solicited from persons wishing to obtain Substitutes, in anticipation of a future draft. We are also prepared to take contracts to fill the quotas of towns, at prices which will make it an object to the Supervisors of Towns to call on us before putting in any men.

All orders filled at this office at as low figures as any other office in Elmira.

Elmira, Dec. 3d, 1864.

A. P. FERRIS & Co.

A. H. FERRIS, B. C. WARD.

SILAS FERRY, WM. DONNELL

References.—John Arnot Jr., Cashier, Chemung Canal Bank, Elmira, N. Y.—Hon. Wm. T. Post, Elmira, Constant Cook, Esq., President 1st National Bank, Bath, N. Y., D. C. Howell Esq., Cashier Steuben Co., Bank, Bath, N. Y. dec3-dtf

Ad for Union volunteers. Elmira *Daily Advertiser,* December 21, 1864.

On December 12 an advertisement promoted the Elmira Skating Park at the corner of Columbia and Clinton Streets– season tickets for ladies and gentlemen $5.00 and children $2.00. "When the condition for skating is good a red ball will be hoisted upon the staff at the Brainard House and a red light at night." Spectators will be admitted for 10¢ "but not to skate." This was where our new LECOM school is under construction.

On December 17 we heard from General Sherman. He said he was a few miles from Savannah and in fine spirits.

On December 19 it was reported that a "Glorious Victory – a great Battle in Tennessee captured 49 pieces of artillery and 5000 prisoners."

On December 21 Elmira Business College advertised upcoming classes in Book Keeping, Penmanship, and Mathematics. "One can complete a course by attending evenings only."

The Union army was still asking for volunteers and substitutes. Over at Constitution Headquarters, in Mansion House on Baldwin Street, was where one could sign up or appoint a substitute to go instead.

The Elmira Skating Park held their Grand Carnival. "Everybody should go, if not to skate, at least to see and be seen." Fireworks illuminated the scene. "One of the most charming and delightful occasions ever known in Elmira."

"Gifts for the Holidays" from Elmira stores included watches, jewelry, silver and plated ware, tea sets, coffee urns, cake baskets, sugar stands, syrup cups, butter, and fish knives, napkin rings, French and American clocks.

On December 22 was Elmira's Firemen's Grand Ball at Concert Hall hosted by Red Rover Engine Company #3. "They got things up in first-rate style."

On December 23 a new doctor – Dr. J. W. Stewart opened offices at 74 Gray Street between Elm and Davis Streets. He was a special doctor. He "can describe and locate diseases merely by the patient's coming into his presence. The Dr. will not touch the patient but be at a distance from him or her. He says he depends on an Invisible Power with which Nature seems to have endowed him." No medicine given or surgical operations performed.

Photography was a popular gift item in Elmira at the time. One could buy cyanotypes, ambrotypes, daguerreotypes, tintypes, and carte de visites. Shops in Elmira included Knowlton"s at 13 and 15 Lake Street over Chauncy Webb's drug store, T. Cendenny opened at 156 Water Street, and J. H. Whitley opened at Lake and Water Streets. A. P. Hart's store was at 22 Lake Street.

On December 24, sugar-cured hams were available at the G. S. Dickenson market at No. 8 Lake Street, along with cod-fish, ground java coffee, butter crackers, and potatoes.

The *Daily Advertiser* wasn't printed on December 25 or 26 but resumed on the 27th.

December 27 reported that the Ladies Hospital Aid Society had provided a "bountiful holiday dinner" for "soldier patients" in the city at the two U. S. General Hospitals – one on William Street and one on Clinton Street. Their bills for the month including food for the Christmas dinner, a stove and furniture for the cook, Robinson & Ingraham whiskey for the Clinton Street hospital, J. K. Perry whiskey for the William Street hospital, a bushel of potatoes, one dozen cabbages, more potatoes and turnips, oysters, chickens, and poultry came to $98.11.

"A much-needed improvement has been commenced at the rebel prison, consisting of the cutting of an artificial channel for the small stream that passes through it, which will have the most beneficial results, not only to prisoners confined there, but the troops quartered there, and our citizens residing in the vicinity of the prison."

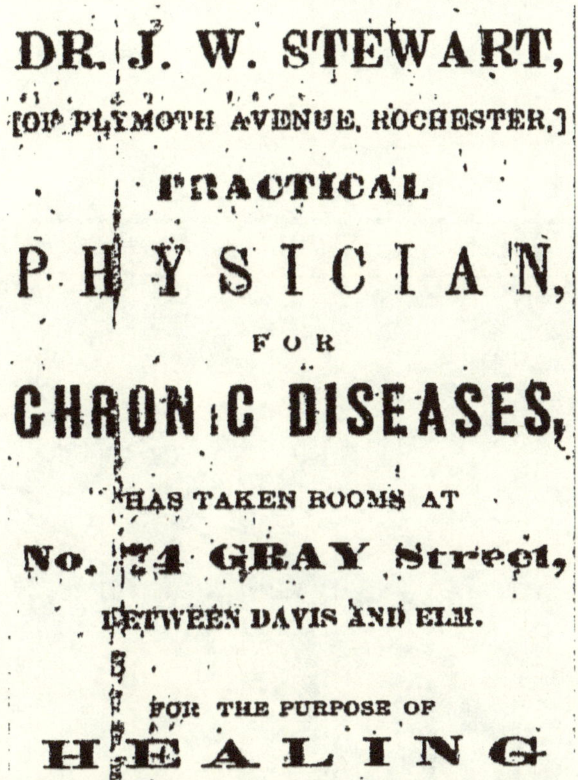
DR. J. W. STEWART,
[OF PLYMOTH AVENUE, ROCHESTER,]
PRACTICAL
PHYSICIAN,
FOR
CHRONIC DISEASES,
HAS TAKEN ROOMS AT
No. 74 GRAY Street,
BETWEEN DAVIS AND ELM.
FOR THE PURPOSE OF
HEALING

Advertisement for Dr. Stewart, Elmira *Daily Advertiser*, December 23, 1864.

"Strayed - a white pig with three black spots on the right side, strayed on Sunday from the premises of the subscriber." 36 Fourth Street in Elmira.

Sources:

Elmira *Daily Advertiser*. Volume, December 1, 1864, Page 1
Elmira *Daily Advertiser*.. Volume, December 7, 1864, Page 3
Elmira *Daily Advertiser*. Volume, December 12, 1864, Page 3
Elmira *Daily Advertiser*. Volume, December 17, 1864, Page 3

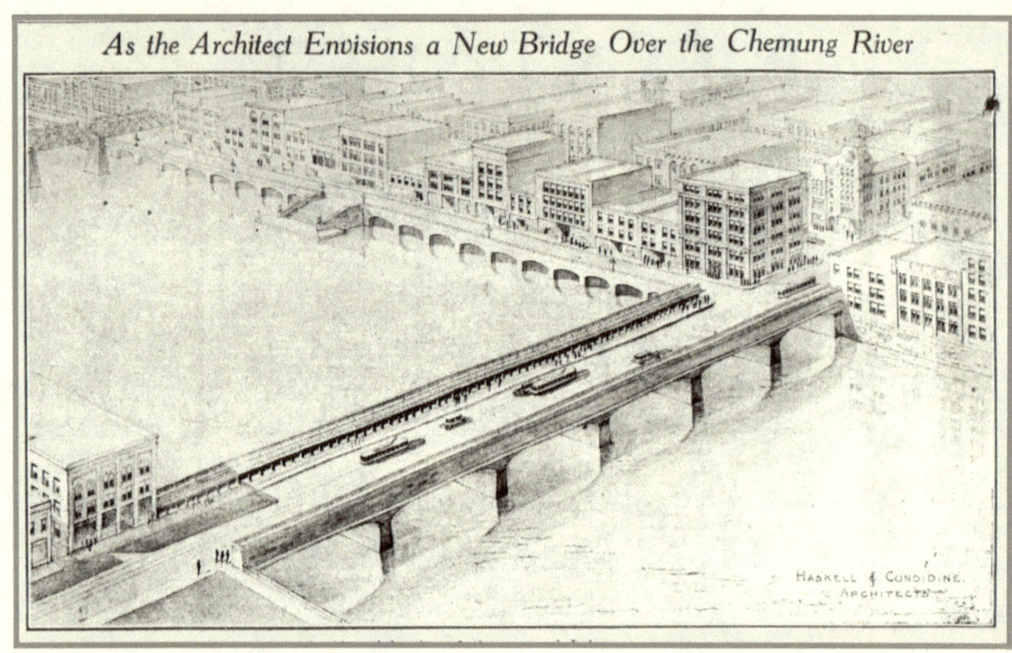

Architects' version of the new Lake Street Bridge. Star-Gazette (Elmira, New York)23 June 1933, Page 8.

Lake Street Bridge

by James Hare

On September 20, 2014, a dear friend and former colleague of mine, Marsha Brown, was featured in the *Star-Gazette*. The headline read, "Activist seeks new life for Lake St. Bridge."

Marsha's vision was to see the bridge, closed in March of 2011, turned into something as beautiful as the Bridge of Flowers in Shellburne Falls, Massachusetts. The article pointed out that she was upset, "to learn city officials say it can't be done...." She was working to build community support to get the city to act.

At that time, the city faced the challenge of how to pay for reopening the bridge. With an influx of state funds in 2019, the money has been found, and plans for a reopening of the bridge will take shape in the Spring of 2020. According to the planning document, "the bridge must first be structurally sound and safe for pedestrians which the project will ensure. Additionally, the project will redesign the space to include benches, lighting, a walking and bike path and railings, and bike racks.

The space will also eventually include a stage for community events and local artistic programs."

Marsha expressed her frustration that things moved so slowly. She noted that "by the time you get around to actually doing something with it, it could be too late." Sadly, Marsha Brown passed away in May 2016.

Visions for the Lake Street Bridge are not new. In 1933, a group of local businessmen, led by J. John Hassett Sr. proposed the demolition of the existing bridge (built in 1905). Their plan envisioned the use of funds from the National Recovery Act. The new bridge would have "eight lanes of traffic provided...outer lanes could be maintained for parking spaces...there would be ten-foot sidewalks for pedestrians."

Also located on the bridge would be 150 enclosed rental stalls on both sides, which would constitute a "central city market." Also, a large plaza was contemplated on the south end on property owned by Hassett, but he was prepared to donate. (Elmira *Star-Gazette*, June 23, 1933)

Like Marsha Brown, Hassett was frustrated in his vision with no state or federal dollars made available. Eventually, repairs were made, and the bridge, built in 1904-5, lasted until 1961 when the current bridge was built.

The importance of the Lake Street Bridge was noted at the time of Hassett's proposal. Sponsors of the project observed that the "Lake Street Bridge is a unit of a through highway route extending from Central Pennsylvania to the Canadian border. The route has been in use for nearly 200 years, being the course followed by pioneer settlers and traders in this vicinity."

Before the building of the first bridge in 1824, there were two ways to get across the river into Elmira. One was to ford the river when it was low enough. It seems hard to believe now, but this seldom happened because the river was deep and rapid at the fording site at that time. According to news accounts, there are records of two or three persons drowned, with their horses trying to cross.

Another way to cross was by ferry, which was operated at the point of the current Madison Avenue Bridge. One ferry operator was John Kline, a German immigrant who ran a "public house" on the north side of the river. The August 25, 1978 *Star-Gazette* noted that "when enough people gathered on the south side to warrant a trip they would shout Over! Over! to Kline. Hearing the call, Kline would shout back Treckly! Treckly! broken English for "directly."

Accounts of the period indicated that Kline did not really mean "immediately."

Agitation for a bridge began around 1810 and seemed to have more interest in the Southside. Over the years, attempts were made to organize a company to build a bridge. On April 16, 1823, the Elmira and Southport Bridge Company was created by law. The Supervisors of the Towns of Southport and Elmira were empowered to lay taxes on the inhabitants thereof for the construction. The first bridge was finished in 1824, made of wood.

The bridge and those that followed made the ferry obsolete. The early bridges charged tolls and indeed experienced a good deal of hard luck. The first bridge had three spans, which sagged over time. One news account reported that a drove of cattle broke through the first span during a period of high water, and both cattle and wreckage were borne away by the swift current.

The first bridge lasted sixteen years until it was extensively damaged by the "great fire of 1840." A covered bridge was built to replace it, but it burned in 1850. Once again, the bridge was rebuilt and stood for thirteen years.

Over that time, it was neglected and became shabby and decayed. In 1863 it was repaired, but disaster struck two years later. The St. Patrick's Day Flood of 1865 washed away most of the bridge.

According to Ausburn Towner, "the only stone pier of the bridge was undermined, and almost the whole of the southern span dropped out and sailed off down the river…it was a great sight to look south across the valley and see instead of meadows, fields, and fences, an immense lake formed there almost in a night."

The early "toll" bridges afforded access over the river but at a price to the Village of Elmira's economy. The toll varied for a two-horse team, a one-horse rig, or a person. The farmers considered it a tax. Many farmers from the Seeley Creek area took their business south rather than pay the toll.

According to an article on file in the Chemung County Historical Society Archives, "there are those who claim that the brisk little village of Troy, in Bradford County Pennsylvania, would never have been except for the bridge."

In 1874, the city erected an iron bridge. It was the first non-toll structure spanning the river. That bridge would be replaced in 1905.

The 1905 bridge was closed in 1959 because of severe structural problems. A new bridge (the one now being considered for redevelopment) was opened on June 21, 1961.

A crowd of between 1,200 and 1,500 gathered to witness the ceremonies.

The *Star-Gazette* reported that "City officials hailed the new structure as "concrete" proof that rumors that Elmira is decaying are false. It was cited as an example of the progress and development in store for the Elmira of the future."

The program ended, the paper reported, "in a scramble for Ping Pong balls tossed from nearby buildings.

The balls were redeemable for merchandise valued at $1000."

The Chemung Canal in Elmira looking north, circa 1860.
Photo in collection of author.

Old Elmira

by Diane Janowski

As a historian, I hear, "Elmira is not the same as it was." Yes, that is true, but every fifty years, one can certainly notice the changes.

During the summer of 1885, The Elmira *Daily Advertiser* ran a 20-plus series of articles about Jonas Lawrence, who was born in Elmira, then Newtown, in 1805. "He grew to manhood in our little hamlet on the banks of the Chemung, was educated in the schools of that day and at a suitable age entered into active business as a merchant, lumber dealer, grain dealer, and shipper." Through his business, he knew many local citizens "up and down the Chemung River and north to the head of Seneca Lake." Jonas came home to Elmira for a visit after 44 years of being away. The changes in Elmira were significant to Jonas.

Back in his day, Jonas took an active part in the Chemung Canal in the 1830s and the New York and Erie Railroad in 1839 and 1840. The railroad went bankrupt in 1841, and Jonas lost his money in the venture. He was forced to "close up his business as best he could, making large sacrifices, and went west to Ohio." Later he moved to young Chicago, Illinois. As Chicago grew and gained importance, "Uncle Jonas," as he was called, became more prominent and prosperous. Over time, his wife died and his children married, and his grandchildren "would climb in his lap" and ask for stories of the old times.

In 1885 Jonas was eighty years old. He loved to tell stories of his Elmira fifty or sixty years earlier. His memory afforded unerring accuracy.

Jonas came back to Elmira on Friday, August 7, 1885, on the No. 12 train to spend several months at his childhood home to "look over familiar grounds and to search for old acquaintances. He is nicely quartered at the home of one of our best citizens (Harry Sampson) on West Water Street, who has promised to spend several months driving our streets, country roads, and visiting villages and towns in the surrounding country."

Jonas was a young businessman when he left Elmira. The *Daily Advertiser* wished people to know that he was back in town to "make your acquaintance and talk over bygones in a friendly manner."

Jonas first wanted to be directed to the corner of Lake and Water Streets. He remembered a tavern on the corner – the owner's name was

Dunn. Dunn had built the first grist mill in Newtown around 1800 and the tavern in 1804. He remembered the tavern as the most popular spot in town.

Jonas remembered that John Arnot had a store on the opposite corner. Harry took Jonas farther down Water Street and showed him the Chemung Canal bank (today's Chemung County Historical Society). They talked about the Arnot family. Harry took him to the home of old friend Lyman Covell who was still alive.

Jonas noted that the old Mechanics' Hall had been replaced. He quoted, "There is not a single building standing here now that was here when I left." This landscape included John Arnot's foundry on the corner of today's Lake and Market Streets. Also gone was Miles Cook's grocery store, and the old Mansion House hotel. All of these places were before photography came to Elmira, so there are no photographs.

Harry told Jonas that the hotel had burned. They talked of the *Advertiser* newspaper and its history. They walked past the new Masonic temple (today's Hazlett building). Jonas had been a mason in Elmira in 1832. He remembered his initiation into the lodge as a sleighing party of the masons where they had crossed Sing Sing Creek in Big Flats, and a sudden wind storm forced the entire group to seek shelter at a nearby farm. He remembered a brisk fire in the fireplace. Out came the "cider and red pepper" and doughnuts.

Upon reaching home in Newtown later in the evening, dinner with "extra fortitude" was taken. That evening continued with talks of raffles, shooting matches, fox and deer-hunts.

Jonas and Harry walked north on Lake Street past the County buildings and the Arnot home (today's Arnot Art Museum). Jonas recalled that when he left Newtown in 1841, "none had predicted to see Newtown or Elmira as a city." He remembered "a big fight" between Newtown and Horseheads and who would get the county seat."

They walked up Church Street. Uncle Jonas was getting tired, but he didn't want to quit. They looked at the First Presbyterian church. They walked down Railroad Avenue to the train station. Harry explained that four railroad companies used the station, the New York, Lake Erie and Western, the Lehigh Valley, the Northern Central, and the Tioga and Elmira State Line.

They walked past Wisner Park, and Jonas remembered it as a cemetery. They saw the Park Church. Jonas remembered Main Street as being called "the back road to Horseheads." He recalled the wheat fields along the road and "frequently you could hear the wolves howl."

They looked at the new Main Street bridge. Harry said, "Yes, Uncle Jonas, this is the Main Street bridge – and it's free, too." Tolls were no longer charged. At this point, they went home to Harry's for dinner.

At dinner, Harry explained that it was the railroads that made Elmira a real city. By the time that the railroad was finished, Jonas had been gone ten years. The completion of the rail line attracted a large number of persons to Elmira, who became citizens. He remarked on those who became wealthy using the railroad to ship their goods nationwide. Harry told Jonas of the railroads south from Elmira to Pennsylvania with its coal mines and lumber.

The next morning Jonas and Harry walked down to the Lake Street bridge to "have a look at Clinton Island." Jonas recalled having some "good times down on the Island." "The grass was as soft as velvet and the shade in the summertime cool, the air refreshing, while the rippling of the waters furnished music that quieted the nerves and it was a resort to which the weary might take refuge." Harry explained that Clinton Island was gone. The owner of the land had cut down all the trees and hauled away its gravel.

Next, they walked down East Water Street to Newtown Creek. They talked of the early settlers and their homes and stores in the vicinity. Jonas asked what the buildings on the hill were. Harry explained they were the Gleason Water Cure.

Jonas remembered the neighborhoods called Pigeon Point and Slabtown. Jonas remarked that "Elmira had erected elegant and substantial school buildings."

They looked at the Elmira Reformatory and the Rolling Mills along the railroad. Jonas remembered the Chemung Canal.

Then they got on a streetcar to see Elmira quicker. They went up to Horseheads that had been called Fairport when Jonas left. They went to Millport, Blossburg, Big Flats, Watkins Glen, and Mansfield.

The series of articles went along for about 20 weeks, and it just disappeared. It took me a while to figure out that the *Daily Advertiser* realized that the Jonas articles would work better as a book. The next year the newspaper published the Jonas articles *Letters of Uncle Jonas Lawrence* as a book that was given out to its subscribers.

Sources:

Elmira *Daily Advertiser*. August 12, 1885, Page 8, Image 8

Elmira *Daily Advertiser*. August 19, 1885, Page 7, Image 7

Elmira *Daily Advertiser*. August 26, 1885, Page 7, Image 7

Elmira *Daily Advertiser*. September 01, 1885, Page 7, Image 7

Elmira *Daily Advertiser*. September 08, 1885, Page 7, Image 7

Elmira *Daily Advertiser*. October 20, 1885, Page 7, Image 7

Elmira *Daily Advertiser*. October 27, 1885, Page 7, Image 7

Construction of the Mark Twain Hotel, dated August 18, 1925. Image courtesy of Allen Smith.

Mark Twain Hotel

by James Hare

In the late 1970s, my wife and I visited the President Calvin Coolidge Historic Site at Plymouth, Vermont. We went to the museum, cemetery, saw the Coolidge Cheese Factory, and toured the family home where Coolidge took the presidential oath, administered by his father, upon the death of President Warren Harding.

Across the street from the family home was the Coolidge birthplace attached to the post office's rear. While attempting to get a picture of that quaint site, I was aggravated by a station wagon that disrupted my photo until I was informed the driver was John Coolidge, the president's son. He was most gracious when I asked him to join me in a picture. He told me that he had been to Elmira and specifically recalled staying at the Mark Twain Hotel.

In a 1963 *Star-Gazette* column, Former County Historian Tom Bryne wrote that the Mark Twain Hotel had "been the city's showcase for nearly 35 years."

He noted that the erection of the hotel at Main and Gray Streets had been talked about for a quarter of a century before opening. Indeed the hotel was memorable. At the opening banquet on March 23, 1929, S. F. Iszard remarked that "As a whole, the Mark Twain is most fascinating to me. I have traveled extensively abroad and throughout the United States, and I have not seen anything in a community of this size to equal it. It is a splendid improvement to Elmira." The *Star-Gazette* of March 24 also recorded other reactions. "I can't believe that I'm in Elmira; many guests remarked. It seems so metropolitan." And "From the outside, the hotel made an impression all its own. Lighted from top to bottom, with the strains of an orchestra floating faintly from the lobby out over Wisner Park, it made people say, Gee, but Elmira is a great town after all."

An article from the vertical file at the Chemung County Historical Society notes that the eight-story building, "included 212 guest rooms, each with a bath; a large main dining room, two private dining rooms, a coffee shop, a ballroom with a foyer large enough to accommodate 350 people for conventions, banquets, and other social functions, a spacious lobby lounge, three elevators of the most modern type and 12 stores and shops on the ground floor."

The Elmira *Advertiser* reported on November 27, 1927, that the prospect of a new hotel being built in Elmira led to an investigative scout being sent to the city by a nationally known industrial organization seeking a site for expansion. In a positive report, some of his findings were: "a population of 52,000, less than 11% foreign, two hundred fraternal and social clubs, forty-two passenger trains daily, fifty churches, one automobile to every four in the county, six theaters and a seven cent trolley fare.

The *Star-Gazette* noted that Attorney J. John Hassett deserved the "lion's share of the honor for making the Mark Twain possible." With Hassett at the helm, Frederic H. Hill, vice-president, and general manager of the Elmira Water, Light and Railroad Company and Arthur B. McLeod, President of the LeValley-McLeod-Kinkaid Company, these three Elmirans comprised the "great triumvirate which directed the campaign for funds and which was highly instrumental in putting the project across."

The sale of bonds raised the million dollars required for construction. Mutual Life Insurance Company purchased $400,000 worth, and Mr. Hassett purchased $300,000, half in cash, and the other by turning over the site, which he owned for the project. The final $300,000 was raised by public subscription. More than 450 Elmirans bid for the bonds in a fundraising drive led by the Wisner Park Corporation, organized to build, finance, and lease the hotel. He newly created Elmira

Hotel Operating Corporation was granted a twenty-one-year lease, and the Lowman Construction Corporation was selected to build the hotel.

A significant obstacle to the whole project was whether or not to widen Gray Street. Citizens opposed the cost, which was estimated at $125,000.

An alternative proposal was to create a new street, approximately 40ft wide from West Gray to West Church Street through Wisner Park just west of the First Baptist Church at the cost of $16,000.

In February of 1928, a city-wide referendum was held. Out of 9,000 eligible voters, 3000 taxpayers voted to reject the plan with a 535-vote majority.

Mr. and Mrs. Hassett decided to convey to the city without cost a "strip of land 17ft wide running easterly from the southeasterly corner of West Gray and Main Streets, 169- feet and a fraction, being a strip 17 feet off the entire frontage of the proposed hotel property." (Elmira *Advertiser* February 29,1928). This reduced the cost of widening the street to approximately $70,000. Ignoring the referendum, the city council voted 8-4 to widen the street. One alderman stated that he did not feel the referendum was a "fair test" of the feeling in Elmira.

Nearly 600 guests attended the opening banquet for the hotel. The *Star-Gazette* reported on March 25, 1929, that, "As a social function the opening festivities surpassed any other similar event of the season and will long be remembered by those who attended."

One glitch, however, was that it was discovered that through "some error" invitations to the official opening were not sent to all persons who were on the mailing list. Those who did not receive an invitation and thought they should have were urged to "get in communication" with the hotel's resident manager.

A banquet at the Mark Twain was special with all it's white linens and a row of silverware on either side of your plate.

Special times!!!!"

Thomas A. Botts, photograph courtesy of Hudson Alexander.

Talking to Elmira Prison Camp Descendants

By Diane Janowski

I live about two miles from the site of the Elmira Prison Camp. I've read all the books. I have no doubts about their facts about the conditions inside the camp. To me, what was missing are the stories of the individual prisoners. What circumstances brought them here?

A second question that bothered me was that many prisoners from the same towns and regiments shared the same last names. I counted sixty- eight instances off my prisoner database. Were they, in fact, brothers, fathers, sons, and cousins? The answer was yes; many were. With 21st century technology, I tracked down some descendant families who were willing to talk to me about this challenging subject.

Answers to my questions were hard-hitting, and what surprised me were the parts of the stories that they neglected to mention to me, or about which they did not know. In many cases, soldiers had become disillusioned by the War. They were absent without leave, intending to go home. In some cases, soldiers were captured by their side and sent back to their companies to continue fighting. They were eventually caught and sent to Elmira.

Of the sixty-eight instances, a few related soldiers were

- David and John Brooks, cousins, 11th Regiment, Georgia – both died on the same day.
- Dennis and Ephraim Evers, brothers, 40th Regiment, North Carolina - died thirteen days apart.
- Alex and Malachi Creekmore, brothers, 15th Regiment, Virginia - died four days apart.
- John, Jesse, and William McWatters or McWalters, brothers,

17th Regiment, North Carolina. William survived Elmira.
- William and Isaac Saddler or Sadler, brothers, 20th Company, South Carolina Volunteer Infantry. Isaac survived Elmira, but he died on the way home.
- Edwin and Elias Smith, brothers, 36th Regiment, North Carolina, both died on the same day.

So how do their descendants pass down their person's legacies today?

John Evans told me of his great-grandfather, Henry Evans of Walton County, Florida. "Those who endured Elmira's squalor and harsh cruelties referred to it as "Hellmira" because of the inhuman treatment. It was a filthy cesspool in summer and frozen in winter. The winter of 1864-65 was one of the harshest on record and unusually cold to the Florida boys. In 1865 the daily ration was reduced to bread and water. Henry suffered from scurvy and dysentery while imprisoned.

Hudson Alexander told me of his great-great-uncle, Thomas A. Botts of Virginia. "He had a mania for buttons--sewn on every available spot of his coat -- hundreds of buttons from every state in the union. You could not put down the point of your finger without touching a button." The Elmira "Yanks" asked him many times about the buttons. After being hard-pressed, Botts told them, "each button was for every time he killed a Yank – and this was his second coat." The last time Botts saw his family and his home was during a brief period between March 6 and April 31, 1862, when military records listed him as "home on leave of absence." Several Botts family descendants speculate that he may have fathered the last of his five children during this furlough. In Woodlawn National Cemetery's plot No. 2801 lies Thomas A. Botts – "Buttons," to those who knew him.

Art Hathcock told me of his great-great-great-grandfather, Calvin Hathcock of the 42nd North Carolina troops. "My great-great-great-grandfather was almost killed at Gettysburg, and again at Fisher's Hill on August 13, 1864. Sadly, Calvin died in the Elmira prison. If I am not mistaken, he was the only one to die from the family during the Civil War. Through my research and opinion, all prisons during the Civil War were very bad and just as bad as the South. My opinion is more so because the North had plenty of food and clothing and did nothing to help its prisoners, unlike the South."

I think that Calvin was still suspicious of me and my intentions, adding, "I hope you honor these young soldiers that were far away from home that never returned..."

I am a life-long resident of Elmira, and, as a historian, I live with the legacy that the name "Elmira" holds. The site of the prison camp and the cemetery are sacred grounds today. I can feel it when I stand there. Tears well in my eyes every time. I visit the boys every month or so.

From Wikipedia: Simeon Benjamin (May 29, 1792—Sept. 1, 1868), founder of Elmira College (NY)

Simeon Benjamin

by James Hare

As an Elder of the church, a major responsibility was maintaining church discipline. An activity seen to be inappropriate for proper Christian conduct was dancing. When it was reported that a church member was dancing at a cotillion party, he was part of a committee designated to visit her. At another point, he was a witness at a Session meeting against Mrs. D. A. Towner, who was seen dancing twice. Mrs. Towner was suspended by the Session and eventually taken off the church rolls.

Who was this man?

Sally Ide Shane, from the Elmira College Class of 1958, as a sophomore in 1955, wrote the following song identifying him.

Verse One *In 1855 when Elmira began*
It was founded by a wise and worthy man
He thought perfection could be designed
If women and books combined

Verse Two *In the years gone by we have grown to be*
Equal to men academically
And as our founders dream unfolds
We seek what the future holds

Refrain *He had a black cloak, a very quiet appeal*
Confidence is a rare ideal
Simeon Benjamin is the name
That began Elmira's fame

According to Sally Ide Shane, this song won the Merry Chanters contest in 1955 and was on the first recording of the "Twelmirans" album in a 1976 letter.

Simeon Benjamin was born on May 29, 1792, in Upper Aquebogue, in the Town of Riverhead on Long Island. He was one of eight children.

According to Ausburn Towner in his *Brief History of Chemung County*, "he was accounted of rather a feeble physical constitution, and was allowed some special advantages for an education which in those days consisted chiefly of extra time from farm work for attendance at the district school, and early initiation into clerkship in a country store in his native town..." Capitalizing on this education, he went to New York City at age sixteen to clerk in a store on Broadway for two years. He returned home two years later to go into business for himself.

With the advent of the War of 1812 and the British blockade of New York City, Benjamin's general store proved to be a bonanza. At the end of the war, he returned to New York City and opened a "first-class dry goods store" at 371 Pearl Street. He operated his store for the next twenty years with great success.

In 1835, Benjamin moved to Elmira hoping to preserve his health. In his pamphlet about Benjamin, written in 1930, Boyd McDowell wrote,

> *"The coming of Simeon Benjamin seems to have been different from that of any other prominent men in the valley. The rest came here with their fortunes to be made... But with Mr. Benjamin, it was different.*
>
> *He had made his pile... Within six months after his arrival, he purchased and paid cash for fifteen different pieces of real estate located on Water, Lake, and Baldwin Streets."*

Being a committed Presbyterian, he quickly became an Elder in the First Presbyterian Church of Elmira, a position he would hold until his death. Over the years, he became President of the Chemung Railroad connecting Elmira with Seneca Lake. Towner credits him with the success of the railroad. He also became Vice President of the Elmira Rolling Mills Company, the largest industry in the town. He was President of the Bank of Chemung and the First National Bank. Civic duties included Fire Warden of the village in 1840 and Assessor in 1846.

In the spirit of reform sweeping upstate New York, he was a supporter of the Temperance movement and an abolitionist and part of the Underground Railroad network.

The concept of a college for women, equal to that for men, surfaced in April of 1851 in Albany, New York, with the organization of the "Friends of Education" at the Second Reformed Dutch Church. By the fall of 1851, plans for a female college in Auburn had progressed enough that the New York State Legislature was asked for a charter. The charter for the Auburn Female University arrived on October 23, 1853. New York State Regents stipulated that before state funds could be requested, the institution had to be up and running, and financially solvent within two years. Because of financial challenges, an alternative had to be considered.

Dr. Augustus Cowles, the first president of the Elmira Female College and a fellow member of the First Presbyterian Church, in his memorial to Benjamin noted that there was some suspicion that the project was a "little radical or visionary, a little too progressive and inclined towards women's rights and female professions."

With the demise of the Auburn project, the proposal was laid before Simeon Benjamin. He donated $5000 to amend the charter to transfer the project to Elmira. He agreed to become the Treasurer and Chairman of the Board of Trustees.

Cowles went on to note that Benjamin "had this new and difficult problem before him for a solution.

How should a new college be established in a part of the State in which higher educational institutions are unknown; a real college for women which shall be higher and better than any female institution in the country." Hank Walshak, in his book *Elmira College, Still Ahead Of Its Time,* noted that Benjamin, "selected a site on Prospect Hill for the massive building that would house the Elmira Female College…one of the most beautiful sites in the village."

The College opened on October 2, 1855, with two hundred forty-two students. Cowles noted that the concept of "charitable aid was prominent."

The cost for a student to attend was $120 per year to pay for all college costs. These included board, tuition, furnished rooms, fuel, and light. The State Legislature appropriated $10,000, which was the first instance of state aid for the "collegiate education of women."

According to Cowles, "The College had been to him (Benjamin) like a lovely daughter of his later years brought up under his fostering care into a beautiful bloom of young womanhood.

He had watched the perils of her birth and infancy. He had liberally supplied her wants, and he had lived to see her command esteem and love of a full circle of friends…." Over time, Benjamin contributed $80,000 to the founding of the College, in the shape of grants, loans forgiven, and a bequest in his will.

In 2019 dollars that equates to $2,355,337.93.

Simeon Benjamin was married to Sarah Wickham Goldsmith of Mattituck, Long Island. They had three sons and four daughters. All but one son and one daughter died in childhood, and the surviving son, William, died immediately after finishing his course at Williams College. The remaining daughter became the wife of the Hon. John T. Rathbun of Elmira. Benjamin died on September 1, 1868.

A New Bridge for Elmira

by Diane Janowski

In 1918, the forty-seven-year-old Main Street bridge was a steel structure 18-feet wide.

It was deemed unsatisfactory, and an order banning heavy traffic over it forced a diversion to the Lake Street bridge. The weight of full-capacity trolley cars to the Willys-Morrow plant, American La-France, and other Southside industries was the cause.

In 1919, more than twenty firms bid for the construction of a new bridge. In August 1919, our Common Council decided that a new structure was needed. The buildings on the north approach would be razed. In the meantime, repairs continued to keep the bridge open. By September 1919, the repairs proved useless, and the bridge was closed. "There were defects in every span."

Elmira needed to be ready for the future. It was predicted that our population would reach 100,000 by 1930. So, we needed a new and better bridge.

By 1920, Elmira was in dire need of a new Main Street bridge. But what kind? Metal or concrete? The Main Street bridge had considerably more traffic than the Lake Street bridge. The Seneca Engineering firm of Montour Falls recommended that many repairs were needed. But what to do? It was the main route for the trolleys and the thousands of employees who worked on the Southside. The Elmira Water, Light, and Railroad Company's equipment were well over the weight limit. Until then, signs of weight limitations were posted. A new bridge was out of the question "until the market improved."

Elmira Mayor George W. Peck said, "Elmira is growing. Its growth cannot be checked. Of course, it is up to the people to deter-

Remainder Of Old Bridge Makes Plunge In Chemung River From Its Supports

The above photograph was taken this morning by The Star-Gazette photographer, who succeeded in getting a picture of the old Main street bridge in midair, after it had been pushed from its supports and before it crashed to the river, breaking into thousands of pieces. The handsome new Main street bridge, expected to serve Elmira for several generations, may be seen in the background.

The last of the old bridge fell into the Chemung River on September 26, 1921. Photo: *Star-Gazette*.

mine how rapidly it will grow. It has been established that the city is growing more rapidly in the western section of the city. That means more traffic for the Main Street bridge."

On January 10, 1920, it was decided to let the taxpayers vote on what kind of bridge they desire.

On February 11, a bridge expert from New York City came and gave his opinion to a "bridge forum meeting." Engineer B. H. Davis told those in attendance that we needed a concrete bridge. He said it was "more durable, more attractive, and an economy in the end." Our mayor at the time, George W. Peck, agreed with him. Davis brought pictures of some of the country's most significant bridges with him – all made of concrete.

On February 17, postcards were received by 9,000 Elmirans, on which they were to state their choice among four main Street Bridge propositions. They had to be received before February 19.

When the results came back on February 20, they were as follows. Total received 4,440. Of these 3,371 voted for a wide concrete bridge, 274 for a narrow concrete bridge, and 159 for narrow steel bridge. Mayor Peck said, "The referendum vote dispels all fear that the small taxpayer would not vote for the best bridge. The referendum has proved a big victory for the Bridge Committee. It is evidence that Elmira is progressing in the right direction. It shows that people have the best interests of the city at heart."

J. Sloat Fassett, former congressman, and resident Elmiran, wanted a "wide concrete bridge, big enough for safety and business, and handsome enough for pride, especially as it is cheapest." The Elmira *Star-Gazette* said if Mr. Fassett, a heavy taxpayer, favors a wide concrete bridge and is perfectly willing to pay a large share of its cost, should now we little taxpayers be equally desirous of contributing our small share both "for business and pride?"

The Main Street bridge's plan was drawn by the Luten Engineering Company with seven piers and eight spans.

Engineer Davis explained that with a concrete bridge, "there is no danger of too much weight...Concrete can withstand greater stress than steel."

Mayor Peck was glad that Mr. Davis had come, as Peck had spent the previous two months ruminating on the question. He had had a "number of conferences with various experts and had studied the local situation from every angle." The mayor advised a bridge of not less than 38-feet wide roadway. He advised a bridge that would meet all future needs.

On May 1, 1920, the old bridge was still closed, and a new one was still in discussion. It was thought that construction would begin about ten days after the contract was signed.

On May 22, Mayor Peck viewed the bridge from an airplane and expressed keen delight from the thrill ride. On May 26, the $360,000-plus contract was awarded to the T. L. Eyre Company, who promised a new bridge by September 15, 1921. Actual work on a new bridge began on June 14.

The first load (900 sacks) of cement for the new bridge arrived in the Southside yard on July 22, 1920. The expectation was 80 train carloads of cement in all.

Construction progressed quickly, and it opened to pedestrians on September 12, 1921. The last remaining pieces of the old Main Street bridge crashed into the Chemung River on September 26, 1921. Only the new structure remained.

Lights were installed on December 8, 1921. Mayor Peck said, "The bridge is the best-lighted location in the city, the two powerful lights on each of the 14 posts on the bridge giving forth a bright white light."

The Main Street bridge was formally opened and dedicated on December 27, 1921.

It lasted until December 14, 1974, when it was deemed unsafe. The new and current one was opened on July 17, 1976.

Sources:

Star-Gazette (Elmira, New York) February 11, 1920, Wed Page 4
Star-Gazette (Elmira, New York) January 16, 1918, Wed Page 11
Star-Gazette (Elmira, New York) June 30, 1919, Mon Page 13
Star-Gazette (Elmira, New York) August 09, 1919, Sat Page 7
Star-Gazette (Elmira, New York) September 27, 1919, Sat Page 2
Star-Gazette (Elmira, New York) May 01, 1920, Sat Page 3
Star-Gazette (Elmira, New York) September 26, 1921, Mon Page 5
Star-Gazette (Elmira, New York) December 08, 1921, Thu Page 2
Star-Gazette (Elmira, New York) February 18, 1920, Wed Page 6

New Keeney Theater Will Open Dec. 21 With Moving Pictures

Image from *Star-Gazette* (Elmira, New York) 04 Dec 1925, Page 24.

Sunday Movies in Elmira

by James Hare

Throughout 1926 a firestorm raged in Elmira over whether or not there should be Sunday movies at the theaters. Chemung County Children's Court Judge Bertram L. Newman was chairman of the opposition.

According to the February 24 *Star-Gazette* he noted that "it is a well-known fact that morally Elmira has a bad reputation…wherever you go you hear comments relative to the immoral condition existing in this city." On November 1, the paper reported that Rev. John Richards, pastor of First Methodist Church, defined the issue, "it is the old, old question of God versus money…the work of the church is made difficult, and that of Sunday school nullified…." The paper also quoted a representative for the youth of Elmira, Kenneth Andrus, who observed that "some say that the parents of the individual boys and girls should judge whether they attend the movies on Sunday.

If the parents are so competent, why do we have to have compulsory education laws?"

At its last meeting on Monday, December 21, 1925, the lame-duck Elmira Common Council dropped a bombshell on the city. With eight Democrats voting "aye" and four Republicans voting "nay," the Council legalized Sunday movies. The action was not a complete surprise and had been anticipated for a couple of weeks. Petitions bearing 2000 names against and 350 for the ordinance were submitted, but no one appeared personally in opposition. (*Star-Gazette*, December 22, 1925) Ironically, the new half-million-dollar Keeney Theater (site of today's Clemens Center) opened that very night with "The Ten Commandments" the first film. The ordinance was to take effect immediately.

State law had long forbidden Sunday movies. However, in April 1919, Governor Al Smith signed a bill that enabled communities to show Sunday movies if desired. (*Star-Gazette,* April 23, 1919). The Elmira Common Council was not at that time inclined to take action. Former County Historian Tom Byrne had written that "the campaign for Sunday movies started March 3, 1920, when the Central Trades and Labor Assembly petitioned the Mayor and Council to allow theaters to open on Sunday so long as it didn't interfere with church services. The working people of our city feel that they should be allowed some form of harmless amusement on Sunday as they are enjoyed by other cities' working people," the petition read." After that burst of energy, the issue disappeared until the Keeney Theater was being built.

With the coming of the new year and a new Common Council, the battle over Sunday movies was joined.

The Elmira Minister's Association, the Young Men's Christian Association, the Billy Sunday Club, and the Virginia Club were in opposition.

As a result of a mass meeting, a Committee of One Hundred was organized to lead the fight.

On January 4, 1926, Alderman Wood M. Rickolt introduced a resolution prohibiting Sunday movies.

While his resolution failed, amendments would be offered to allow Sunday movies between the hours 2-7 pm and 8:30-11 pm and one calling for a referendum at the general election in November.

Throughout January and February, public meetings were held to debate the issue.

At the February 1 hearing, the *Star-Gazette* reported that, "apparently 19,000 residents of the City of Elmira, more than five hundred in person, and 18,500 represented through petitions gathered in the assembly chamber of City Hall Monday evening to voice opinions as to whether or not Elmira should continue to have Sunday motion pictures."

THE NEW THEATER.

Elmirans had their first opportunity to view the interior of the fine new Keeney Theater yesterday, and as they thronged out its doors after both performances, words of praise were on every lip.

It is a metropolitan playhouse, to the last detail. Capacious in size, decorated in fine harmonious taste, equipped with every convenience and comfort for patrons' use and centrally located, it is a credit to the city.

Elmirans can well be grateful to the men whose enterprise and means made the new theater possible and added this imposing structure to the long list of large public edifices in this city.

Frank A. Keeney of New York, the lessee for a long term of years, received a warm welcome from the evening audience, and many kindly words also were spoken of George H. Vendemark and Malcolm D. Gibson, the well known Elmirans, who are to manage the playhouse.

The Keeney Theater will be one more busy center of high class entertainment, and is one more positive indication that Elmira is a metropolitan city.

WHAT'S NEXT?

Sunday movies are to be permitted hereafter, by decisive vote of the Common Council.

One long step having been taken towards a less restricted Sunday, what will be the next step in that direction?

Star-Gazette (Elmira, New York) 22 Dec 1925, Page 6.

Judge Newman expressed concern that one more temptation would be placed in front of the children.

The Rev. E. M. Merring, the pastor of the Hedding M.E. Church, spoke for half an hour on the character of the Sabbath, "Sunday is an isle of safety in the midst of the scramble of modern life.

The world requires a period of rest.

On that day, in so far as possible, all work should cease." One speaker referred to the so-called "Continental Sabbath," the seventh day as it is observed in Europe, as the "evil root." From that, he claimed, came difficulties related to World War I, diplomatic intrigues, non-payment of debts to the United States, and free use of liquor. In South America, he stated that carelessness about the Sabbath led to high illegitimacy rate and the people are both immoral and non-progressive.

Albern Johnson, leader of the Seventh Day Adventists, opposed repeal to unite church and state.

> *"I am in favor of religious liberty, and the present matter is purely a religious proposition. Back of the whole matter lies the desire to enforce Sunday observance by religious law...We don't want a civil government sending people to church at the end of a policeman's club...any church that needs a crutch of civil law to help it along is sadly in need of power."*

In response to Judge Newman's petitions with 7,500 signatures in favor, Thomas Grant Welsh presented 10,799 cards bearing signatures in favor of Sunday movies.

Their legitimacy was challenged by Rev. John Richards of the First Methodist Church and Rev. Salvador Musso, the Italian Mission's pastor.

At the public hearing held on February 15, Judge Newman opposed a referendum as making the Sunday movie question political.

Rev. C. G. McConnel of Centenary Methodist Church challenged the cards presented by Mr. Welsh, stating that only 2,277 had proved to be voters.

Attorney William H. Mandeville defended Mr. Keeney, stating that "he had no intention of thrusting anything down the throats of Elmira. He came here with a view of pleasing Elmirans."

On February 24, the *Star-Gazette* noted that "enthusiasm for Sunday movies in the city on the part of the majority of theater owners had lessened." At the council meeting that night, the Common Council voted seven to six to rescind the Sunday movie ordinance until a referendum was held. Democratic Mayor David N. Heller was the deciding vote.

The referendum vote was twelve to one with Alderman Rickolt opposed.

Throughout the summer, the debate raged. The Committee of One Hundred mailed out 10,000 letters urging people to register to vote. Rev. John Richards warned that, "the cross which you place opposite the word No will be a symbol of the crucified Son of God."

On Tuesday, November 2, 1926, Elmira went to the polls. Nearly 19,000 persons cast ballots on the question. There were 10,820 in favor of Sunday movies and 8,020 against. Eight out of twelve wards voted yes. On Monday, November 15, nine members of the Common Council and Mayor David N. Heller voted in favor of an ordinance permitting showing Sunday motion pictures in Elmira. Three Republican Alderman were recorded as not voting on the proposition.

An 1872 image of Tom Taliday by photographers Moulton & Larkin for use by Scribner's *Monthly*. Courtesy of the author.

A Voice from the Past

By Diane Janowski

I didn't know this until this week, but one of us Elmirans graced the pages of Scribner's *Monthly* - Volume 4 June 1872 to be exact. The article was called "Traveling by Telegraph, Northward to Niagara."

My story starts with finding an old photograph that turned up on eBay. It was an Elmiran with a name I had heard before. I knew I had to have that photo.

On the back of the photo was written "Tom Taliday." I remembered the name from several old Chemung County history books. Although he was the city's "town crier," he is remembered in these books in less-than-appealing terms. I won't repeat the names used to describe him or the things Elmirans did to him.

I knew I had to write a story about Tom because I can't let him go down in history for what we said about him more than one hundred and fifty years ago.

There had to be a back story. Who was Tom Taliday? How did he come to Elmira and become our town crier? Our history books don't mention his family circumstances, but I have a "need to know" curiosity.

Part of researching local history involves making sense of whatever little information is available. I don't always find the whole story, and in this case, I didn't, but I can explain more of Tom's situation than my historical predecessors.

I started my research on Ancestry.com, knowing he must have had a mother and a father, and I found them fairly quickly. That gave me a better idea of where geographically to start on my search.

Tom's grandfather, Hendrick Taliday of Dutch descent, was born in Red Hook, New York, in 1765 and died in Wysox, Pennsylvania, in 1813. History books list him as a pioneer of Wysox - arriving probably as a land grantee after the Indian wars in northern PA. His brothers also settled in the area. Tom's father, John Taliday, was born in Kinderhook, NY, in 1790 and died in Elmira in 1850. His mother, Naoma, was born in Pennsylvania in 1789. It was Tom's father that brought the family to Elmira. There were four children; Tom was the oldest born in 1809 either in Painted Post or Poughkeepsie, depending on the sources I found. He had a sister Sarah and brother John Wilfred, both born in Buffalo and another brother Bartholomew born in Painted Post. Tom and his brothers all served in the military. His brothers all received honors, but Tom had four circumstances that unfortunately ended in his court-martial in 1840. His military records did not explain what happened, but that he was drummed out in Buffalo.

Tom suffered from a medical or mental condition. Elmirans bullied him for it both on the street and in history books.

Tom carried a bell that he rang when a fire broke out, if a child went missing when a storm was coming, and for whatever reason when townspeople needed to be notified. I can't find him having an actual position in Elmira. Maybe he was self-appointed. The census and the city directories list him as a laborer. He lived with his mother on Dewitt Avenue near the river. She died in 1860. Now alone, Tom lived for a while at the Hathaway House on the corner of Lake and Market Streets.

Tom frequently hung out at the Erie Railroad station. On an unusual occasion, a staff member of Scribner's Monthly came through town writing an article about upstate New York. When this writer got off the train in Elmira, there was Tom. The writer was so intrigued by him that he included him in the article. The writer needed a photograph of Tom. Tom had his image taken by local photographers Moulton & Larkin on Lake Street, and it was sent to the author. Someone drew his picture, and it was used in the magazine. The photo I purchased on eBay was probably not the original but a facsimile thereof. Tom goes down in history as being the only Elmiran to grace the pages of Scribner's *Monthly*.

Tom had no money, so his stay at the Hathaway House did not last long. He became a resident of the County Poor House in Breesport. Tom Taliday died in February 1873 and is buried without a marker in the poor house cemetery.

CHAUTAUQUA TO PRESENT COMEDY PLAY

"Crossed Wires," Delightful Comedy-Drama at Swarthmore Tent Tonight—Secretary Redfield Gives Instructive Talk.

Image from *Star-Gazette* (Elmira, New York)15 Aug 1923, Page 2.

Swarthmore Chautauqua in Elmira

by James Hare

The *Star-Gazette*, on August 7, 1923, announced that, "The Swarthmore Community Chautauqua, guaranteed by 100 prominent Elmira businessmen, will come to Elmira Friday, offering a delightful educational and entertainment program through Thursday, August 16. The big tent will be situated on the lot at West Sixth Street and College Avenue, directly opposite the Elmira College observatory. Elmira College gave the location." A special memorial service in honor of recently deceased President Warren G. Harding would take the usual opening.

The word "Chautauqua" in the Iroquois language means either "two moccasins tied together" or "jumping fish."

Whatever its precise meaning, the word describes a lake in western New York near Jamestown. In 1874, John Heyl Vincent and Lewis Miller rented the site of a Methodist camp meeting to use in the post-camp season as a summer school for Sunday school teachers; this became known as the Chautauqua Institute. By the last decade of the nineteenth century, the Institute was nationally known as a center for rather earnest, but high minded, activities aimed at intellectual and moral self-improvement and civil involvement. (www.chautauquatrail.com)

The Chautauqua Movement grew out of this effort but never had a formal relationship with the Institute.

According to the website, "Chautauqua had a degree of cachet and became shorthand for an organized gathering intended to introduce people to great ideas, new ideas, and issues of public concern."

After 1900 the "circuit Chautauquas" became the principal expression of the movement. By 1915, some 12,000 communities had hosted a Chautauqua. Even before 1900, Winter Chautauquas had been held in Elmira. The Elmira *Advertiser* reported that "Large Crowds" had attended programs at the Park Church in February of 1898.

The Swarthmore Chautauqua was founded in 1912 by Paul M. Pearson as a non-profit enterprise financially banked by private investors, many of whom were Quakers. Its purpose was to provide cultural and educational enrichment. According to George J. Dillavou, in his "Life Cycle of an Adult Education Enterprise," report on the Swarthmore Chautauqua, it eventually reached into approximately 5,000 towns and villages each year, and in 1925 the total aggregate attendance was reported at 35,449,750."

The Swarthmore offering in Elmira was one of several appearing in the Elmira area at that time.

It was noted that the program in smaller towns would not be as complete as the one presented in the city. Twelve hundred seats were available, and more could be accommodated. It was anticipated that there would be good attendance as there had not been anything similar held here for several years.

The memorial services which opened the week's events were held at 3 o'clock Friday afternoon to coincide with funeral services scheduled in the dead president's hometown in Marion, Ohio. Congressman Henry F. Rainey of Illinois was the main speaker.

The program lasted an hour and featured the Loren Bates Musical Company singing, "Lead Kindly Light."

That evening at 7:30, the second program opened with Congressman Rainey once again the main speaker and the Loren Bates Musical Company returning to the stage. The *Star-Gazette* on Saturday, August 11, noted that "Loren Bates, in addition to giving the audience the benefit of his splendid tenor voice, provided many laughs with comedic character sketches. The company offered a program of very high quality."

The Chautauqua program's schedule was to begin at 3 o'clock each afternoon and 7:30 in the evening.

At 9 am each morning, a special Junior Chautauqua for children was featured. The children would perform a pageant "Her Family on Display" at 2:30 pm the Chautauqua's last afternoon. The pageant was a characterization of "The Old Woman Who Lived In A Shoe."

A variety of entertainments filled the schedule. On Saturday, the Ruby Gall Light Opera Revue performed twice, and the lecture was on "Crime and Punishment." Vesper services were held Sunday evening, open to the public at no charge. On Monday, a poet lectured on "A Poet's Gospel of Good Will." That evening, the Swarthmore company presented "The Taming of the Shrew." The *Star-Gazette* reported on Tuesday, August 14, that "Elmirans like plays and other theatrical performances in summer perhaps a bit better than lectures and similar kind of entertainment was suggested Monday evening in the big audience that filled the...tent to see the presentation of "The Taming of the Shrew"...the audience was much larger than on either of the other two nights that the Chautauqua has been here. The performance was very capably given and won much applause."

The Tuesday programs featured the Stallings Toy Company. Louise Stallings was a mezzo-soprano soloist with Mr. Ernest Toy, a violinist of note, and Mrs. Toy the accompanist. William C. Redfield, Secretary of Commerce during the Wilson administration, spoke on "We and the World."

Wednesday evening, the night before closing the Chautauqua experience, the company presented the comedy-drama "Crossed Wires." The play was announced as being specially written for Chautauqua in a prize contest conducted the year before.

It was one of 300 plays to be submitted.

The *Star-Gazette*, on the following day, observed that the play and cast "would have a promising chance to win success on Broadway, no doubt, should the effort be made."

It would appear everyone was tired after the Chautauqua closed. The headline for Friday, August 17 was, "Chautauqua Ends Program."

The children's pageant received no comment; the evening program "Cartoons and Comedy Review," was "entertaining." The tent was being dismantled, and they were gone, hoping to return in 1924.

CHAUTAUQUA ENDS PROGRAM

Concludes Entertainments at Tent With Alton Packard, Cartoonist, and Musical Company.

Image from *Star-Gazette* (Elmira, New York)17 Aug 1923, Page 24.

View of the Assauer home in 1877, corner of Pennsylvania Avenue and Spaulding Streets. Image courtesy of the author.

Christian Assauer's House

by Diane Janowski

I found a photograph dated 1877 of an old mansard-roofed house with "Christian Assauer" written on the back with a date but no address. I was hoping that I could make a then-and-now comparison with the current house. It was most definitely a home of an affluent person. Under close inspection with a magnifying glass, there is a stately older gentleman in the middle, surrounded by a younger couple with two children, and an older woman. Another gentleman is seemingly mowing the grass. A big parrot in a cage is in the front yard. I guessed that it was in the Near Westside neighborhood because of its grandiosity.

I called my friend, realtor Shane Searfoss, who knows everything about old and new houses in Elmira. He said that there aren't many mansard homes left locally and that he did not recognize it. So, my Plan B was to figure out its location. The city directories between 1875 and 1897 listed Mr. Assauer at 215 Pennsylvania Avenue. Old maps showed that yes, there it was in all its glory – where Monro Muffler is today.

A quick search for Christian Assauer found that he was born in Germany in 1817 and came to New York City in 1846. After his first wife died, he married his second wife, Mary, and moved to Elmira and sold real estate.

I believe Christian Assauer is the stately man in the center, maybe his daughter and son-in-law next to him, his niece and grandson. I can't guess the older woman's or the smiling lawnmower's relationships.

So what became of that big beautiful house?

In the early days, this stretch of Pennsylvania Avenue was part of the Sly farm in Southport. Many elegant homes lined this street. On the corner of Sly and Maple, pioneer John Sly built his home in 1795. Pennsylvania Avenue joined Sly Street about a block south. It was known as the Plank Road or Toll Road and went all the way to the Pennsylvania state line. Pennsylvania Avenue was a toll road constructed from planks so that farmers would not have to drag their wagons through the mud on the way to and from Elmira. It lasted from 1848 to the late 1880s.

In 1876, Spaulding Street opened to Pennsylvania Avenue. Previously it had only stretched between Catherine and Miller Streets. Between Pennsylvania Avenue and Catherine Street was a vacant lot. Earlier maps showed a house on the lot, but it must have burned down. Eminent domain claimed the lot to complete Spaulding Street.

Assauer was one of many men who owned several property pieces in the area, including the vacant lot. Assauer was very lucky as his house was now a desirable corner property. In 1889 Mr. Assauer lost his second daughter and, in 1893, his second wife. He had this big house, yet he was all alone. A niece came to live with him. Mr. Assauer died in 1897, leaving an estate worth over $50,000 [or $1.5 million today]. It went to his nieces, nephews, and grandson. His live-in niece, Carrie Hart, got the house. The house eventually passed out of the family. In the years after his death, many families had called the address home.

The last mention of Christian Assauer in local newspapers was December 14, 1994. His former property tract on Lormore Street was being sold.

The old house was still there in the city directory of 1968. The Hartman family owned it. Urban Renewal got it around the time of the flood. I am not sure when its demolition came, but the property was foreclosed upon in 1979 and went to the city of Elmira.

Monro Muffler moved from Diven Plaza to Mr. Assauer's lot on Pennsylvania Avenue in December 1982 and is still at that location.

Closeup view of Christian Assauer. Image courtesy of the author.

Sources

Star-Gazette (Elmira, New York) July 30, 1917, Mon Page 6

Star-Gazette (Elmira, New York) December 27, 1982, Mon Page 12

Star-Gazette (Elmira, New York) · Tue, October 19, 1897, · Page 7

HERE THEY ARE ELMIRA...

Twelve New Alleys Open Tomorrow

Image from *Star-Gazette* August 12, 1938.
The opening of Dixie Bowling Alley.

Bowling in Elmira

by Diane Janowski

I grew up watching Syracuse Bowls on WSYR on Sunday afternoons with host Joel Mareiniss in the 1960s. Once in a while, an Elmiran would be on. I learned exotic-sounding towns around Syracuse, as Baldwinsville, Camillus, Solvay, Dewitt, and Mattydale. There were no bowlers in my family, so I can't explain my fascination with the sport. I've gone bowling maybe three times in my life, and the last time I bowled a 71. I don't think that was a good number.

The first mention of bowling as a sport in our area was in the Elmira *Gazette* on February 17, 1842. The article explained the finer points of the game, and that one could really study another's character at the bowling alley. The author spoke of "the way a man measures the alley with his eye," and how the "a man's game of life has been the same as his game of ten pins."

In the early days, bowling was an outdoor summer sport.

In 1893, the Glen Springs Hotel in Watkins Glen had a bowling alley. Corning had an alley in the Windsor Hotel. Elmira had lanes in the Singerhoff building on East Water Street. Waverly had one in the YMCA. Elmira Heights had one in 1896.

Colonel D.C. Robinson had one at his home on Maple Avenue. The Armory, next to City Hall on East Church Street, installed a bowling alley in 1898.

The Kanaweola Bicycle Club installed an alley in their clubhouse on East Church Street in 1899. Stancliff bowling alleys on State Street opened in 1911.

The sport lost favor for a little while in the 1910s and 20s, but by the 1930s, many Elmirans played. Factories, businesses, and churches all had their teams. In a 1932 newspaper, the DL&W (Delaware Lackawanna & Western Railroad) Engineers vs. Yard Dept. Passenger Station vs. Round House, Car Dept vs. Maintenance. The Eclipse factory on upper College Avenue had the Grays vs. the Colonels and the Barons vs. the Senators. The City League had Coca-Cola vs. Cadillac Car, and the Polish Americans vs. BPOE (the Elks Club). In the Industrial League, we had Kennedy Valve vs. Phoebe Snow, Thatcher Glass vs. Kennedy Hydrants, LaFrance vs. Willys-Knight. In the Church League, it was the Synagogue vs. Centenary Methodist.

Also, in the 1930s, the Recreation Bowling Alley at 114 State Street was sold and repaired. The Stancliff Bowling Alley on Baldwin Street was still going strong.

In 1936, Tony Rossi built an alley behind his bakery on West Washington Avenue. Elmira City Council heard from many neighbors about the possibility of too much noise coming from the establishment. In the end, the council sided with Rossi, and his alley opened in August 1936. The Oakwood Bowling Alley also opened in 1936.

The *Star-Gazette* reported on August 12, 1938, that the Dixie Bowling Alley opened with the idea to encourage "women bowlers." At their establishment, "women will find a private lounging room where they can rest and change into their bowling togs." Local clothing and shoe stores did a rousing business in bowling shirts and shoes.

In the 1940s, many (under-aged) Elmirans found jobs as pinsetters as the old alleys were not mechanized. Most were employed without the knowledge of their schools or parents. Truancy was a big issue. It was reported that 4 out of 5 pin boys in New York State were working illegally under Child Labor Laws. 53% of Elmira's pin boys were underage.

Automated alleys came into fashion around 1944, but Elmira's alleys didn't get up to speed until the 1950s. Dixie was automated in 1956. Paramount Lanes opened in 1957.

In 1961, the Brunswick Corporation, the maker of the automated bowling pinsetters, requested that the term "bowling alleys" be retired and changed to "bowling lanes."

The year 1962 was Elmira's heyday of bowling. A new bowling alley opened on the southside – the Elmira Bowling Center boasted 52 automated lanes. It was reported that 2,039 women bowlers were registered in local leagues.

Some excellent bowlers in Elmira's history are Frank Carey, Tony Rossi, Seth Winner, Don Reidy, Lynn Hamlin, Debra Drabinski, Ted Nickerson, and many hundred more.

Interest in the sport waned, and in July 1993, Elmira Bowling Center closed. Paramount Lanes closed recently due to the Coronavirus. Dixie Lanes and Rossi Lanes are expected to open at the governor's discretion.

ALLEYS ON MOVE—The six upstairs bowling alleys at Rossi's were pulled out yesterday to later be placed on the ground floor of the renovated hall. The picture (taken looking east from George Washington School) shows two cranes hefting 10 tons of expensive lanes. The 24 alleys at Rossi's will be on one floor by next fall, as will the Dixie lanes at Bulkhead where six new alleys are being constructed.

Image from *Star-Gazette* July 13, 1954 Renovation of Rossi Lanes.

Looking down Watercure Hill Road from the Gleason's Watercure. Photo courtesy of the author.

Mark Twain Walking Around

by Diane Janowski

Historians sometimes lie awake at night, thinking about things. I, myself, spent several nights thinking about Mark Twain, or as we called him in Elmira, Samuel Clemens. Sam, his wife Olivia (Livy), and his family spent twenty summers at Quarry Farm, just up East Hill. Starting in 1871 and ending in 1903, although I doubt he traversed the hill in the later years.

I got to thinking what his wife might have sent him to the store to get. Butter, eggs, milk, or cereal? No, I decided that Quarry Farm was a working farm, so they had their milk and butter as did every other farm. It probably had its chickens, so no need to go out for more eggs. Not to mention they had an excellent cook, Katy Leary, and she probably had charge of the groceries or at least ordering the groceries. And they were perhaps delivered, so Sam really wouldn't have had to pick up any food items.

Then I thought, what would Sam have needed from the hardware store? Sandpaper, screws, nails? No, Quarry Farm already had a handyman, John Lewis, and he probably bought whatever was needed at the farm.

Michelle Cotton, formerly of the Chemung County Historical Society, wrote a book called "Mark Twain's Elmira" that recalled all the stores and places in Elmira during Sam's time. But would he have gone to all those places? I don't think so, and I don't think he would have a reason to shop downtown. He traveled the world, and I don't think he bought his clothes here. He may have purchased paper, pens, and pencils. So probably yes to an office supply store. He liked cigars, so perhaps a tobacco shop.

We do know that Sam enjoyed an occasional cocktail after work. That is true. And he enjoyed the company of others, especially those down at Klapproth's tavern on Lake Street. The building was still there in my childhood.

Then I got to thinking about how Sam would have gotten to Klapproth's from Quarry Farm. Google Maps says it is a distance of 2.4 miles, and a 48-minute walking trip according to the route it mapped for me. But is that the route he took? Might he have come down my street?

So, Sam would have left Quarry Farm probably in his white linen suit, and leather-soled shoes, and walked down the hill passed the Gleason Watercure on the right and Thomas K. Beecher's house on the left. Don't forget it is a steep hill where he would come down. Quarry Farm's altitude is 1480 feet; downtown Elmira is 856 feet. So, Sam would descend and ascend 624 feet on a round trip, in slippery-soled leather shoes. And, the ascension part was after having a drink or two.

At the bottom of the hill, would he have zigged and zagged through the streets of the Eastside as Google Maps suggests? Or did he turn left on Tuttle Avenue then right on East Church Street and come up straight? Or did he follow the Junction Canal to Lake Street? I thought he might have followed the Delaware, Lackawanna, and Western tracks, but that railroad company didn't come to Elmira until after Sam's time.

Klapproth's tavern was located at 162 Lake Street, the site of today's Five-Star bank. The tavern was considered an excellent place for gentlemen; even the Rev. Thomas K. Beecher checked in occasionally for a pint. Klapproth's also sold tobacco products, making it a two-in-one stop for Sam.

So, then I thought about Sam getting home. Did he walk back the 2.4 miles, including a steep climb after a drink or two? Or perhaps a nice Samaritan with a buggy drove him at least partway home? This we will never know.

Klapproth's burned in a fire in February 1968. Some artifacts remain in possession of Elmira College's Center for Mark Twain Studies.

Samuel Clemens came back to Elmira for good in April 1910. He is buried with his family at Woodlawn Cemetery.

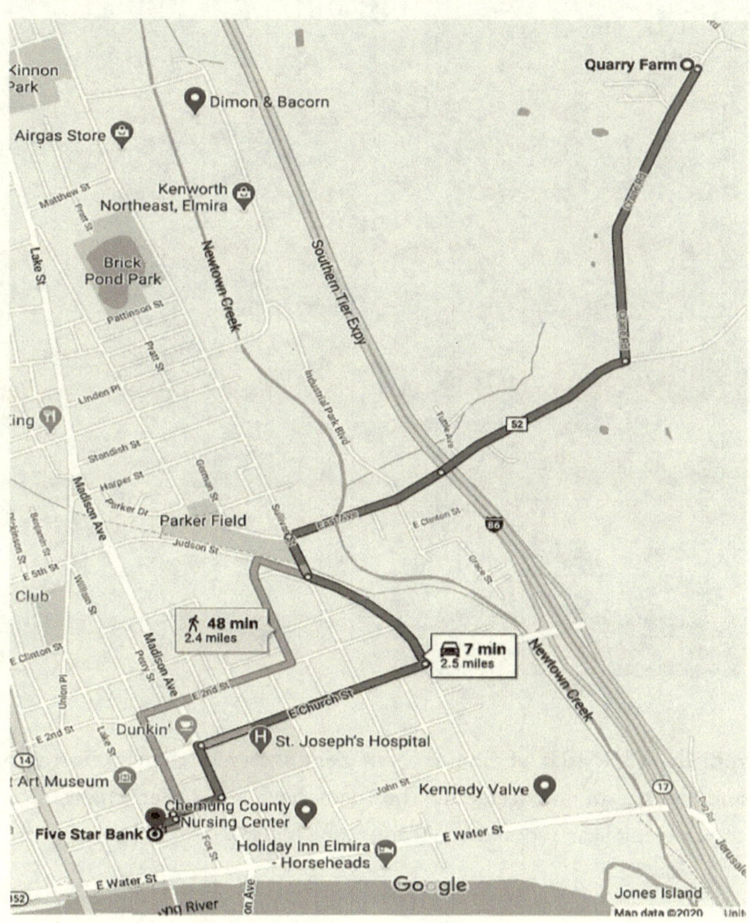

Google Maps' suggested route.

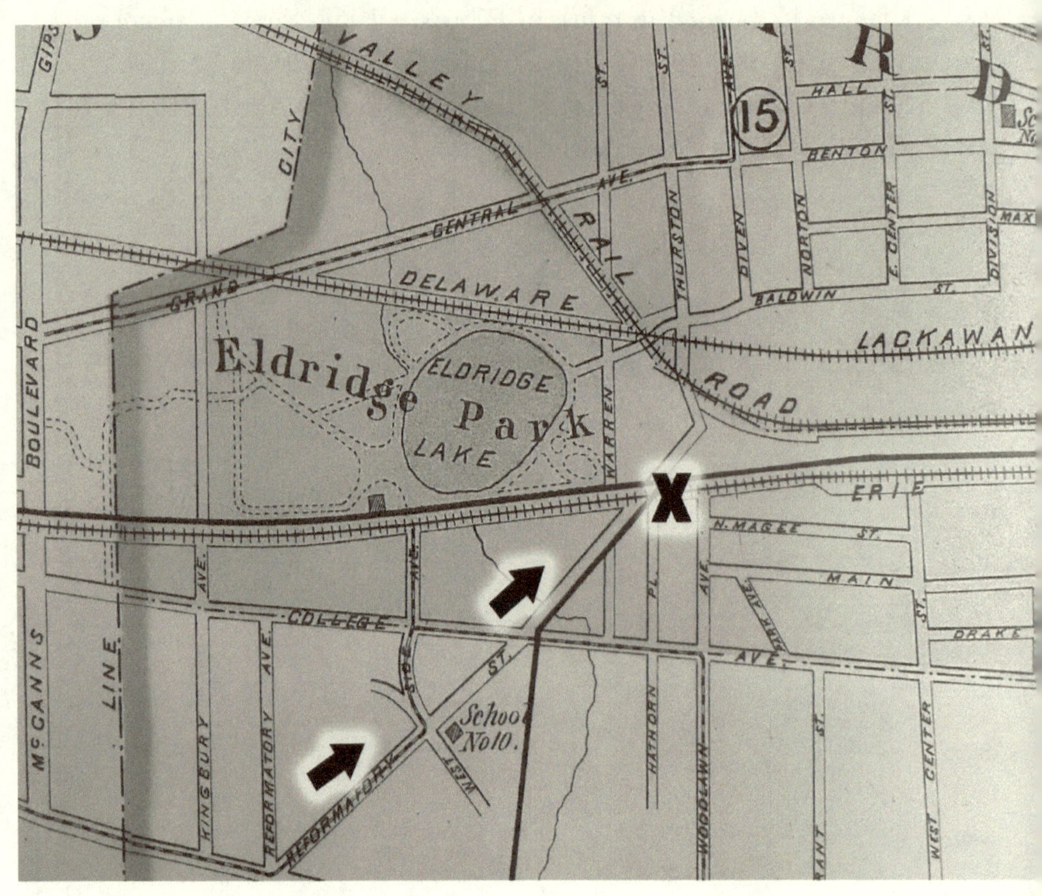

Map from the 1896 atlas of Elmira, New York showing (then) Reformatory Road and the site of the accident. The roads have since been changed, and today the crossing is at Woodlawn Avenue, one block south.

A Terrible Day

By Diane Janowski

On July 27, 1891, forty-year-old Reverend Wellington White and family were on sabbatical from their lives as Christian missionaries in China. They were temporarily staying with his parents on Grove Street. Rev. White hired a horse and two-seated canopy-topped carriage from W. A. Gildea, a local liveryman. White took his mother and sister out for a ride. They returned home at 5:30 PM. While he still had "time on the horse," he rounded up his wife Mary, three daughters, their nanny, and a friend of the children, and left the White home to go on a summer late afternoon ride to Eldridge Park. Everyone was excited about the idea.

All seven rode in a carriage with one horse. The carriage sauntered through Elmira's northside. Near the Reformatory turned right at Reformatory Road (today's West Thurston Street used to connect to East Thurston Street near the main entrance to Eldridge Park). Now East Thurston connects to Woodlawn Avenue at that point (the railroad tracks). For a carriage to get to the main entrance of Eldridge Park, it was necessary to cross the Erie tracks and several of the Delaware, Lackawanna, and Western tracks. It had taken about 30 minutes to get from home to this point.

As they got closer to Eldridge Park, Erie train No. 24 was bearing down from the north. "The train was running a terrific rate of speed."

As the group got closer to Eldridge Park, the horse cleared the tracks, but the carriage did not. Mr. White, daughter Lillian, little friend Hattie Hastings, and 14-year-old nanny Susie McCarthy were instantly killed. Mrs. Mary White and daughters, Mabel and Mary, were terribly injured and thrown about. The horse was not hurt. The carriage was in a million splinters.

The train "ran a long distance before it stopped. The train backed up to the scene of the disaster, and in a short time, a large crowd had collected from [Eldridge] park and rendered what assistance they could. The sight which greeted the passengers was horrible. Mr. White lay dead forty rods from where the carriage was struck. Mrs. White lay on the crossing, unconscious while the children lay scattered around, three of them mangled and dead, and the other two maimed and moaning with the pain."

The folks killed were loaded onto the train and brought to the Erie depot. The injured were loaded into a passenger car. Mrs. Mary White and daughter Mary were taken to Erie station's "private room for ladies." Daughter Mabel, who was the least injured, cried "piteously."

Hundreds of people had gathered at the station. The ambulance arrived at 7:00 PM and took the injured to the Arnot-Ogden hospital. Coroners arrived at the depot and assessed the fatalities. Lillian White died of a fractured skull, as did Hattie Hastings. Mr. White died of a dislocated neck and fractured skull. Susie McCarthy "sustained a complete fracture of the skull."

Conductor Ford and Engineer Wynn were terribly affected. Wynn never engineered again.

An eyewitness, M. J. Murray, explained that the carriage was attempting to cross the tracks between an already stopped train split for street traffic. As the carriage passed through the split train, No. 24 coming down the eastbound track, hit it directly in the middle. Murray did not recall if 24 had blown its whistle. He believed Rev. White did not see the train.

Murray said help was there since the second it happened.

Another witness, Mrs. Mary Baxter, who had been standing at the crossing, did not notice the fast-moving train. She turned at the sound of the crash and saw confusion. She also did not hear a whistle.

At the hospital, doctors could not tell how badly Mrs. White was injured, as her eyes were so very swollen. Little Mary had a "terrible scalp wound and a fractured skull." She was given ether for her pain.

Reverend White and family had only been in Elmira since July 1. They were staying with his parents at 503 Grove Street. The White family was to have gone to China "in a few days" to resume their missionary work.

On August 1, Mrs. White partially regained consciousness. By September 11, she was able to sit up. She remained in the Arnot-Ogden hospital until September 14 when she moved to a specialized hospital in New York City. On October 3, she came back to Elmira for a visit. On November 9, she was back in New York. Doctors said her "memory is defective" and has problems with train whistles. She remained in New York with her brother.

On August 8, 1891, the official inquest of the situation gave two verdicts - one citing Mr. White "that through the careless actions of the driver of the vehicle [four came to their deaths], and the other verdict [was] that the train was going too fast. It was recommended that the street be lowered and the tracks raised in the future.

The next year on May 9, 1893, Mrs. White's lawsuit against the Erie Railroad began, citing the danger of the 4 or 5 lines non-gated tracks without a flagman. She also cited that trains were going 40MPH while the city speed limit was 15MPH.

Three days later, on May 12, 1893, Mrs. White won the lawsuit and was awarded $5,000 the limit. She planned to sue for each daughter, though I did not find any more newspaper mentions of it.

As bad as this accident was in Elmira's history, an even worse accident occurred at the Erie Railroad's Pennsylvania Avenue crossing one year later, instantly killing a family of five.

Sources:

Star-Gazette (Elmira, New York) July 28, 1891, Tue Page 5

About the authors and this book series....

Diane Janowski is the current Elmira City historian. She is also the editor of *New York History Review,* and was formerly the editor of the *Chemung Historical Journal.*

She has written many books about Elmira and Chemung County history, and co-authored the book *Images of America, The Chemung Valley* with Allen C. Smith.

James Hare is a retired teacher of American History and Government from the Elmira City School District. He is also a former mayor and councilman for the City of Elmira.

He co-authored the book *Images of America, Elmira* with former county historian J. Arthur Kieffer.

Hare and Janowski are freelance writers for the Elmira *Star-Gazette.* Since 2014, they each write monthly articles on the history of the city of Elmira, New York. This book is a selection of their articles.

www.ingramcontent.com/pod-product-compliance
Lightning Source LLC
LaVergne TN
LVHW051010080826
845145LV00009B/2558

* 9 7 8 1 9 5 0 8 2 2 0 9 6 *